Demons
and
Rabid Dogs

GEORGE O. ADEBANJO, Th.D.

ISBN 979-8-89269-049-2

To my daughter Nicole, grandson Xavier, and my wife Jennifer –
Thanks for being partners in my life's journey.

Table of Contents

PREFACE

The book "**Stray Dogs and Demons**" was first written and self-published in 1996. This publication is an edited copy of the original but also a combination of new material. Also included are materials from other publications such as "Thank God for Deliverance", "Discerning Spiritual Attacks" and Spiritual Warfare workbooks. It is intended to share my knowledge in spiritual warfare as well as encourage those currently struggling in warfare that they are not alone.

"Ye shall not need to fight in this battle: set yourselves, stand ye still, and see the salvation of the LORD with you, O Judah and Jerusalem: fear not, nor be dismayed; tomorrow go out against them: for the LORD will be with you" (**Second Chronicles 20:17, King James**).

Spiritual warfare can become overwhelming and sometimes lead to disillusionment which causes some to ask questions if God really cares.

The word of God speaks of increased demonic activities in the end of times, and this truth is more evident in the twenty-first century than at any other time. So, my purpose is to share my knowledge of spiritual warfare with my readers.

In the past, I had many questions about demons, and the spirit-world. Frankly speaking, I still have questions, but the Lord has given me answers and insight into a lot of things including living a victorious life during a fierce battle which has caused some to fall. This book will empower the readers with the necessary information, and I believe that you will be blessed, and enlightened by being open-minded as you read this book. Finally, there will be distractions due to the activities of "**seducing spirits**" but stay focused and experience the victory through Christ and the knowledge of His Word.

"Now the Spirit speaketh expressly, that in the latter times some shall depart from the faith, giving heed to seducing spirits, and doctrines of devils (**First Timothy 4:1, King James**)

INTRODUCTION

"For we walk (Live) in the flesh. We are not carrying on our warfare according to the flesh and using mere human weapons. For the weapons of our warfare are not physical weapons) of flesh or blood). But they are mighty before God for the overthrown and destruction of strongholds" (**2 Corinthians 10:3,4**)

Andrew B. Law was almost correct by saying that, **"There is no such thing as an inevitable war. If war comes it will be from failure of human wisdom"**. However, there is another kind of war that is solely directed at God loving Christians. No Christian is exempt from it, and it is best to learn about it and be dressed up for battle.

This warfare is not a new conflict, for it started in heaven as written by Apostle and beloved disciple.

"And there was war in heaven Michael and his angels fought against the dragon; and the dragon fought and his angels And prevailed not; neither was their place found any more in heaven. And the great dragon was cast out, that old serpent, called the Devil, and Satan, which deceiveth the whole world: he was cast out into the earth, and his angels were cast out with him" (**Revelation 12:7-9**) KJV.

This warfare had been fought by many of God's children and is still ongoing. This kind of warfare has no physical battleground, nor can be fought with natural weapons, because this warfare is between Christians, demons and fallen Angels.

The main difference between fallen angels and demons is that demons are disembodied spirits whereas fallen angels have bodies, there is hierarchy with both demonic and angelic spirits. That is, they are highly organized.

"For we are not wrestling with flesh and blood (contending only with physical opponents) but against the despotisms, against the powers, against (the master spirit who are) the wicked rulers of this present darkness, against the spirit forces of wickedness in the heavenly (supernatural) sphere" (**Ephesians 6:12**).

In accordance with this warfare, Paul instructs Pastor Timothy to:

"Endure hardness as a good soldier of Jesus Christ: that he may please him who hath called him to be a good soldier" (**Second Timothy 2:3,4**).

One of the characteristics of "**good soldiers**" is to be "**disciplined**" and follow the instructions of the officer in charge and the vision of the Commander in Chief. Good soldiers know that effective warfare requires that one learn about the enemy's weapons and tactics. They know that it is imperative to be watchful, alert, and sober during warfare. It is also imperative for good soldiers of Christ to know that believer's warfare cannot be won with conventional weapons. In addition, this warfare cannot be prevented by arms treaty or War Powers Resolution. This war must be fought with the right kind of weapons in order to live a successful Christian life. There should be no doubt in our hearts as to the validity of this Warfare.

Warfare Is Real!

It is a spiritual warfare which started in heaven, and we are the targets of demons and fallen angels who have been expelled with the devil from the City of angels.

"And there was war in heaven: Michael and his angels fought against the dragon; and the dragon fought and his angels and prevailed not; neither was their place found any more in heaven" (**Revelation 12:7,8 KJV**).

These fallen angels are ranked as "principalities, powers, rulers of darkness..." (**Ephesians 6:12**). Demons also have ranks, but unlike fallen angels are assigned to torment, harass, and distract believers in a clandestine form so that fingers are pointed to other people rather than the original source. It is important to remember that demonic attacks are directed at the believer's faith in order limit the walk of faith. Jesus warned Peter of the devil's desire to attack Peter's faith.

"And the Lord said, Simon, Simon, behold, Satan hath desired to have you, that he may sift you as wheat: But I have prayed for thee, that thy faith fails not: and when thou art converted, strengthen thy brethren (**Luke 22:31,32**).

Prayers and fasting are necessary for effective warfare against demonic forces. The basic operations of demons is through deception and are recognized by their activities. For example, seducing spirit is the name attached to demonic spirits who are exponentially active in the twenty first century because of the end time prophecy by Apostle Paul.

"Now the Spirit speaketh expressly, that in the latter times some shall depart from the faith, giving heed to seducing spirits, and doctrines of devils; Speaking lies in hypocrisy; having their conscience seared with a hot iron; Forbidding to marry, and commanding to abstain from meats, which God hath created to be received with thanksgiving of them which believe and know the truth" (**First Timothy 4:1-3 KJV**).

In addition to "**seducing spirits**" the bible also credits Satan and his demons with blindness and dumbness as revealed in the gospel according to Matthew.

"Then was brought unto him one possessed with a devil, blind, and dumb: and he healed him, insomuch that the blind and dumb both spake and saw" (**Matthew 12:22, KJV**)

However, all blindness and dumbness are not the consequence of demonic activities. Research shows that blindness affects many people around the world, and no one should be dogmatic to associate demonic attacks to all cases of blindness.

In addition to the connection of blindness to demonic attack. Dr. Luke also ascribes the deformity of a woman to the work of Satan, for Jesus said, "And ought not this woman, being a daughter of Abraham, whom Satan hath bound, lo, these eighteen years, be loosed from this bond on the sabbath day?" (**Luke 13:16**) KJV.

Increased demonic attacks in various shapes and forms should not come as a surprise to those who are students of the Word of God. Jesus tells us that, Satan is a "**thief**" whose agenda is:

"**To steal, and to kill, and to destroy**" and to cause pain to many. Apostle Paul wrote, "This know also, that in the last days perilous times shall come. For men shall be lovers of their own selves, covetous, boasters, proud, blasphemers, disobedient to parents, unthankful, unholy, Without natural affection, trucebreakers, false accusers, incontinent, fierce, despisers of those that are good, Traitors, heady, high minded, lovers of pleasures more than lovers of God; Having a form of godliness, but denying the power thereof: from such turn away" (**Second Timothy 3:1-5, KJV**)

Demonic attributes are quite evident from the above scriptures. Notice words such as "proud", "**unholy**", "false accusers", etc. are not listed among the Fruit of the Holy Spirit. Therefore, are ascribed to demonic influence.

Believers have been given the assignment to generate positive influence in the world through the power of the Holy Ghost. Apostle Paul reminds Believers that born-again believers are in a far superior position than unclean spirits and fallen angelic beings because every born again believer resurrected with Christ "and made us sit down together - giving us joint seating with Him in the heavenly sphere...Far above all rule and authority and power and dominion, and every name that is named above every title that can be conferred not only in this age and this world, but also in the age and the worked which are to come" (**Ephesians 2: 2,6**).

What an awesome opportunity and provision given to every follower of Christ to be seated with the Messiah, the sacrifice for the sin in the throne room where nothing can hinder experiencing His love and power. Jesus Himself says,

"Behold, I give unto you power to tread on serpents and scorpions, and over all the power of the enemy: and nothing shall by any means hurt you. Notwithstanding in this rejoice not, that the spirits are subject unto you; but rather rejoice, because your names are written in heaven" (**Luke 10: 19,20 KJV**).

Does the enemy have any power? He would like for us to think that he has none, and that he really does not exist. If the devil has no power and is nonexistent, there would be no murderers, rapists, drunkards, devil worshippers, backsliders, incestuous crimes, racism and the list goes on. However, his influence on Christians is limited, based on your relationship with the "**Father of lights**" provided we "**walk in the light**". This means that, God the Holy Spirit will reveal what is in darkness because the Word of God is "a lamb unto my feet, and a light unto my path" (**Psalms 119:105 KJV**).

Total surrender to the Holy Spirit will activate the promised power that has been given to each believer.

Chapter One
The Beginning

I was about the age of eight when I had my first puppy. Surprisingly, I was able to hide it from my father with the cooperation of my other siblings. That was until one day, our father came home unexpectedly, and both my father and the dog startled each other. My dog growled at my father and the puppy ended up at dog pound to be seen no more. Guess what? I cried because my pappy got rid of my puppy. The memory of my puppy stayed with me till I grew up. I couldn't wait to grow up so that I could have another puppy or dog that no one could dispose of. Fast forward, upon traveling out of Nigeria the opportunity came to have four-legged family friends.

Some of my four-legged friends came from the dog pound, some were given to me, some were bought, and others chose me as their friends. The latter were Stray dogs. A stray dog becomes your friend, as long as food is provided.

Demons have some things in common with stray dogs. Demons will stick around if they are fed, and similarly stray dogs will also stick around as long as they are fed. Yes, demons do eat. They don't eat steak, mashed potato, or any natural human food. What then is demon's favorite food? Hosea writes,

"They eat up the sin of my people, and they set their heart on their iniquity" (**Hosea 4:8**).

"They" refers to unclean spirits who feed on sinful behaviors. These evil spirits also known as demons are in partnership with the flesh for their sustenance, and survival. Any unscriptural acts, sacrifices, or rebellious behaviors and works of the flesh provide feeding frenzy for demons among other things.

"And they shall no more offer their sacrifices unto devils, after whom they have gone a whoring. This shall be a statute forever unto them throughout their generations" (**Leviticus 17:7**).

In every generation many people are ignorant of the level of deceptions that emanate from the kingdom of darkness. For example, in ancient Egypt were those who considered dogs to be divine and were mummified. Also, in India are those that believe that they are related not only to dogs, but other creatures including cows, snakes, and other animals through reincarnation.

"They provoked him to jealousy with strange gods, with abominations provoked they him to anger. They sacrificed unto devils, not to God; to gods whom they knew not, to new gods that came newly up, whom your fathers feared not" (**Deuteronomy 32:16,17 KJV**).

These "new gods" are fallen angels and demon spirits who through deception receive worship from those who are ignorant. An ignorant and wicked woman in the bible who worshipped idols was judged by God using dogs as the instrument of divine judgement.

"And the dogs shall eat Jezebel in the portion of Jezreel, and there shall be none to bury her..." (**Second Kings 9:10**). The above prophecy was literally fulfilled in verses 35 through 37 of Second Kings chapter nine. These wild dogs however did not consume her skull, feet, and hands.

Consumption of humans for medicinal purposes is another deception of Satan. The author of Medicinal Cannibalism in Early Modern English Literature and Culture, L. Noble, and others such as Richard Sugg of England University of Durham point out that, "**for several hundred years, peaking in the 16th and 17th centuries, many Europeans, including royalty, priests and scientists, routinely ingested remedies containing human bones, blood and fat as medicine for everything from headaches to epilepsy**". Fast forward to the 21st century, money rituals which involve human sacrifice are practiced through demonic deceptions.

Corpse eating is one of the doctrines of demons that is practiced in ritual worship. One of the many Hindu deities, Shiva is worshipped in northern India by a reclusive religious sect called The Aghori. They live close to the cemetery. Their place of meditation is the crematorium where Hindus burn dead bodies. This place is considered to be home to ghosts and evil spirits by Hindus, but Aghori sadhus prefer to live and meditate there. In general, other Hindus prefer to stay away from Aghoris.

Elijah the prophet stayed away or rather ran far away after being threatened by the queen. Jezebel was the idol worshipping evil queen in the bible that was not only blood thirsty, but vindictive, and controlling. Demons control people when ignorant of what happens at death. There are so many places around the world that people pray to the spirits of their ancestors. Dr. Koch points out "that Japan among other countries, practice the worship of their ancestors. The Japanese continue to pray to the spirits of their ancestors and to offer sacrifices of food to them, while spiritistic cults contact and address the spirits of the dead." These are familiar spirits that can imitate the voice of a departed dead and God forbids communication with the dead.

"Regard not them that have familiar spirits, neither seek after wizards, to be defiled by them: I am the LORD your God" (**Leviticus 19:31**) KJV

"Don't make yourselves disgusting to me by going to people who claim they can talk to the dead" (**Leviticus 19:31)** Contemporary English Version.

"And when they shall say unto you, Seek unto them that have familiar spirits, and unto wizards that peep, and that mutter: should not a people seek unto their God? for the living to the dead?" (**Isaiah 8:19**) KJV)

Communication with dead opens up portals to the world of spirits that ultimately will bring unnecessary problems to one's family. The bible reveals the unfortunate event of a king Saul who was inspired by God to ban the practices of Witchcraft from Israel. However, he became vulnerable and therefore was opened to deception by demons. In his desperation and vulnerability decided to travel to Endor in order to find answers from a medium.

"Then said Saul unto his servants, Seek me a woman that hath a familiar spirit, that I may go to her, and enquire of her. And his servants said to him, Behold, there is a woman that hath a familiar spirit at Endor. And Saul disguised himself, and put on other raiment, and he went, and two men with him, and they came to the woman by night: and he said, I pray thee, divine unto me by the familiar spirit, and bring me him up, whom I shall name unto thee. And the woman said unto him, Behold, thou knowest what Saul hath done, how he hath cut off those that have familiar spirits, and the wizards, out of the land: wherefore then layest thou a snare for my life, to cause me to die? And Saul sware to her by the LORD, saying, As the LORD liveth, there shall no punishment happen to thee for this thing" (**First Samuel 28:7-10**) KJV.

The consequence for King Saul's action was severe, for his kingdom suffered defeat, and worse his three sons died, along with the rest of his family. Finally, Saul and his armor bearer committed suicide. Then the enemy dishonored his memory by cutting off his head and displayed it in the temple of Dagon (**First Chronicles 10:1-14**).

Apostle Paul warns, in the epistle to the Galatians, "Be not deceived; God is not mocked: for whatsoever a man soweth, that shall he also reap" (**Galatians 6:7**) KJV.

This should serve as a warning to not take God for granted. Saul, a man chosen by God died like a wicked person because of persistent rebellion. He was anointed to be king, but his actions worked against the anointing upon his life and was judged in his wickedness and as a wicked person along with his household. Wickedness is associated with the wild dogs of the East and prophetically to those who tormented, mocked, and crucified Christ, the Anointed One.

"For dogs have compassed me: the assembly of the wicked has enclosed me: they pierced my hand and my feet." (**Psalm 22:16**).

Dogs Are Perceived Differently In Many Regions Of The World.

For example, in South Korea and Southeast Asia, the four-legged friends are unfortunately used for food consumption. Also, in China and in United Kingdom, dog for consumption is allowed with restrictions. In parts of West Africa, they are used for medicinal purposes. Mark Alizart, writes that, "**In Nigeria, for example, people often eat dog meat in order to cure malaria. In addition, some people believe that the fat from dog meat has medicinal benefits that can alleviate body aches.**"

Mr. Alizart may be making a general statement because most Nigerians do not subscribe to dog meat. However, the reference may be of a particular tribe in Nigeria. In Central America, dogs are allowed to run freely, and sometimes approach humans for food. In the West, dogs are adopted as pets and treated as part of the family. In my opinion, some dogs live better and treated better than humans in the western hemisphere. They can be spoiled and can act worse than a spoiled child. Dogs have been known to be jealous and sometimes growl when ignored out of jealousy. It is not strange for a dog to growl but it is definitely strange when a growl comes out of a man.

During a deliverance session, one of the victims have been seen and heard to growl like a dog. Those present were shocked because he was a church person, actually a Christian. Dogs growl for different reasons such as when afraid, threatened or communicating a warning of a bad intension about to happen, play time is over when a dog growls and similarly, growling out of a person an indication of demonic presence that are afraid of being exorcised. The implication is not that all dogs are possessed but that demons can imitate different emotions for communication including a growl.

As an experienced pet owner who has been around different breeds including Saint Bernard, Great Dane, German Shepherd, and mixed breeds. Their names do not reflect either their breed or personality. The Saint Bernard was named Turkey; the Great Dane was named Peppy. Other names include Lucy, Ajax, Django, and Tiger. Demons, unlike domestic dogs, are not to be played with or even fed. Many people ignorantly play with demons through horoscope reading, Ouija board playing, and calling the psychic network. Demons do eat. The food they eat are unholy and other bad behaviors of their human host or victim. For example, demons of anger and rebellion feed on the emotional pains, misunderstandings, and memories of past hurts, of their victims. Whenever a person continues to dwell and act on a painful memory of the past is an opportunity for associate demons to torment the individual. The primary supplier of the food that demons eat is the human host. Also, every time one reacts in revenge to other people's actions opens the door for the associate demons to feed. It is important to clarify that, being a host does not imply demon possession. A possessed person is never a Christian, however a church person who is not a Christian is a candidate for possession. Moreover, possession implies complete control of the body, soul, and spirit of a person. Demons can never be housed in the spirit of a true believer, but demons can hide in the human flesh or in the soulish area of a Christian, provided the individual Christian does not want to grow and refuses to change. These demons, when fed like stray dogs, will not want to leave, and prefer to stay hidden. No one likes to be associated with hosting these "unclean spirits." However, the reality is that hosts play a harmful role that cannot be ignored. Demons can also hide in the soulish area because the mind is the battleground between the flesh and the spirit. The mind is a complicated part of mind that is subject to renewal or reprogramming. In Paul's letter to the Romans he says,

"And be not conformed to this world: but be ye transformed by the renewing of your mind...." (**Romans 12:2**) KJV.

An unrenewed mind becomes "**the devil's workshop**" and many remains the same with old habits because of the ignorance on the importance of mind. To be transformed is to be changed and changes requires work on self. Just as dogs can be trained to do many things, the human mind can be trained through the power in the Word of God to bring about changes. The gospel has power to effect changes for "It is the power of God unto salvation."

There are two separate parts of salvation. The instantaneous and the progressive aspect of it. This means that when a sinner accepts Christ as Savior, the person is instantaneously a child of God. However, the same person must grow in the Lord as indicated in Petrine epistle.

"Wherefore laying aside all malice, and all guile, and hypocrisies, and envies, and all evil speaking, As newborn babes, desire the sincere milk of the word, that ye may grow thereby" (**First Peter 2:1,2**) KJV.

Growing Into Spiritual Maturity Is A Process. Never Instantaneous!

As in the natural, so also is the process of spiritual growth into maturity of a believer. Everyone in the natural starts with infancy to becoming a toddler, then to adolescent, puberty and finally adulthood. A newborn believer starts drinking "**milk**" before being able to digest solid food. It is as the saying goes, you must "**crawl before walk.**" It is a process that brings about change and growth.

"For when for the time ye ought to be teachers, ye have need that one teach you again which be the first principles of the oracles of God; and are become such as have need of milk, and not of strong meat" (**Hebrews 5:12**) KJV

Change can sometimes be painful: "Though he were a Son yet learned he obedience by the things which he suffered" (**Hebrews 5:8**) KJV. Some call it "**growing pains**", but there is the grace of God as a believer desires the necessary change. "But grow in grace, and in the knowledge of our Lord and Saviour Jesus Christ." (**Second Peter 3:18**) KJV.

There are times when deliverance may be necessary. However, complete deliverance may take a few steps and a few sessions accompanied with counseling depending on the situation of the individual. Prayer is the foundation to deliverance and prayer for deliverance must be understood to be different. There are different types of prayers.

First, a request for protection from transference of demons from the person seeking deliverance to others is important. Second, it is not advisable for those praying to close their eyes. Third, the prayer of deliverance usually takes the form of command. Fourth, it is better to have two people who are in one accord to perform any deliverance.

There are situations when an emergency deliverance can be performed without assistance. When demons unexpectedly manifest. For example, a young person in my car while driving suddenly started growling like a dog. The command was issued to the demons to STOP, and the growling stopped. Demons like dogs understand authority when exercised. Dr. Luke narrates an event that took place in the Synagogue when a command was issued to demons to exit a man.

"And in the synagogue, there was a man, which had a spirit of an unclean devil, and cried out with a loud voice, Saying, Let us alone; what have we to do with thee, thou Jesus of Nazareth? art thou come to destroy us? I know thee who thou art; the Holy One of God. And Jesus rebuked him, saying, Hold thy peace, and come out of him. And when the devil had thrown him in the midst, he came out of him, and hurt him not" (**Luke 4:33-35**) KJV.

Demons can be vengeful by trying to cause harm to the one seeking deliverance. This is one of the reasons why deliverance should not be done solo except in case of an emergency. The assignment to set people free was issued in pairs of two.

"And he called unto him the twelve and began to send them forth by two and two; and gave them power over unclean spirits" (**Mark 6:7**) KJV.

The two must be in agreement in the process of setting the captives free. Think of a household where the wife says to a dog, "sit!" and beside her is the husband saying "come!" to the same dog. The dog will be confused and could actually take advantage of the owners. Demons like to explore disunity to their advantage.

"Can two walk together, except they be agreed?" (**Amos 3:3**) KJV

The Power of agreement can never be over emphasized in churches, and homes. There are all kinds of agreements in the physical sense that are binding. These contractual agreements provide legal protection for the parties involved. Similarly, there are spiritual protections under the New Covenant for those who accept Christ as Lord and Savior. This seal of the agreement is the Blood of Christ. This is why, heaven becomes energized when there is unity of purpose and Believers are in one accord.

"Again, I say unto you, That if two of you shall agree on earth as touching anything that they shall ask, it shall be done for them of my Father which is in heaven. For where two or three are gathered together in my name, there am I in the midst of them" (**Matthew 18:19,20**) KJV.

It is therefore not strange for demons to work overtime to bring about division and confusion in many homes as well as in the Body of Christ and in the nations of the world. It has been said that "a house divided cannot stand!" Consider a situation where a family decides on a three-day fast for a particular purpose. However, unknown to the family were those who did not fast because fasting translates to starvation.

Christians seeking deliverance from demons need to understand that one of the most effective and lasting methods is to STARVE them out! This simply means, stop feeding them! Stray dogs leave when you stop feeding them. Similarly, demons can be starved out when they are not fed any longer.

Initially, there may be difficulties such as with a drug addicted person who has chosen to starve the demons out by quitting the habit. A drug addict that is trying to kick the habit usually will have withdrawal pain. However, with the right support system such as, support group, prayers, fasting and meditating on the Word of God will make it easier to starve the demons out.

There is no easy way out once entrapped by demons. For those who find it difficult to starve demons out there is another option.

The other option is to ask a deliverance minister or someone who is qualified to cast them out of you. There are not many people in the body of Christ who are in the deliverance ministry. This is because demons often will try to take revenge on the deliverance minister or their families for being exorcised from their hosts or victims. They are not always successful with a direct attack on the deliverance minister, but physical attacks of infirmity are sometimes a possibility on vulnerable members of the deliverance minister's family. In addition, many do not take time to learn how to deal with demons. They are like wild pit bull dogs!

Another word of caution is that the deliverance once performed must be maintained, otherwise the demons can return not as before but stronger. This word of caution came out of Christ Himself.

"When the unclean spirit is gone out of a man, he walketh through dry places, seeking rest, and findeth none. Then he saith, I will return into my house from whence I came out; and when he is come, he findeth it empty, swept, and garnished. Then goeth he, and taketh with himself seven other spirits more wicked than himself, and they enter in and dwell there: and the last state of that man is worse than the first. Even so shall it be also unto this wicked generation" (**Matthew 12:43-45**).

Jesus clearly tells us in the above scriptures that demons that have been cast out desire to return and can return.

Therefore, maintaining one's deliverance is important. In the natural, it is necessary to perform maintenance. Homeowners know that the lawn has to be maintained; sweeping, vacuuming and dusting are all part of maintenance. Car owners also know that it is less expensive to do preventive maintenance such as oil and filter changes than to wait until something breaks down. Quarterly visitation to the dentist is also part of preventive maintenance without which more expensive procedures such as dental implant may become necessary. Medical profession recommends that African American males over age 40 are supposed to visit their Physicians for Prostate screening yearly as part of preventive actions that can prevent future disruption in life.

Similarly, a person that has been a victim of demons must do certain things once the person becomes delivered from demonic bondage. In addition to demonic bondage, there are also religious and fleshly bondages. These can be connected to demons but are not the same. Our focus is how to maintain your deliverance once delivered from demonic bondage.

There are several preventive maintenance steps to mitigate the return of demons such as being accountable (**Hebrews 13:17; Jas 4:7**), putting on the whole armor of God (Ephesians 6:10-18) and fasting also helps (**Mark 9:29**) in addition to rejecting ungodly thoughts (**Philippians 4:8; 2 Corinthians 10:5**).

The support of a local church is important for those who are under demonic attacks or have been delivered. Every church may not be equipped to give the necessary support and may need to outsource the needed help to another church that is more equipped. However, it is easier said than done because there are leaders who have the fear of losing the "church member" who needs help. Therefore, will resist the idea of outsourcing the necessary help. It has been said that "no one is an island."

"We then that are strong ought to bear the infirmities of the weak, and not to please ourselves. Let every one of us please his neighbor for his good to edification" (**Romans 15:1,2**) KJV.

The "weak" includes those who are easily swept away, easily offended, and perhaps temporarily or permanently depart from the faith for different reasons.

"Now the Spirit speaketh expressly, that in the latter times some shall depart from the faith, giving heed to seducing spirits, and doctrines of devils; Speaking lies in hypocrisy; having their conscience seared with a hot iron;" (**First Timothy 4:1,2**)

One of the doctrines of demons is that there is nothing called demons, and that Christians cannot be influenced by demons. Another doctrine of demons is to reject tithing as an Old Testament doctrine and claim the exemption of Christians from tithing through an act of deception.

Among those deceived are, Judas Iscariot, Alexander the coppersmith, Demas (**Second Timothy 4:10**) and of course Peter, who denied Christ as well as Judas who betrayed Him.

"And supper being ended, the devil having now put into the heart of Judas Iscariot, Simon's son, to betray him" (**John 13:2**)

Alexander the coppersmith was used by demons to hurt Paul:

"Alexander the coppersmith did me much evil: the Lord reward him according to his works: Of whom be thou ware also; for he hath greatly withstood our words (**2 Timothy 4:14,15**)

Finally, Peter denied Christ three times and realizing his error wept.

"And when they had kindled a fire in the midst of the hall, and were set down together, Peter sat down among them. But a certain maid beheld him as he sat by the fire, and earnestly looked upon him, and said, This man was also with him. And he denied him, saying, Woman, I know him not. And after a little while another saw him, and said, Thou art also of them. And Peter said, Man, I am not. And about the space of one hour after another confidently affirmed, saying, Of a truth this fellow also was with him: for he is a Galilaean. And Peter said, Man, I know not what thou sayest. And immediately, while he yet spake, the cock crew. And the Lord turned and looked upon Peter. And Peter remembered the word of the Lord, how he had said unto him, Before the cock crow, thou shalt deny me thrice. And Peter went out and wept bitterly" (**Luke 22:55-62**).

Chapter Two
A Growling Demon

My first exposure to deliverance ministry was very accidental. It was on a Saturday morning with about ten other Believers who were in the outreach ministry. We usually pray before every outreach including hospital visitation, or door to door witnessing. This time, something unusual happened. I heard a familiar sound – a growling sound. (At that time, I was the proud owner of three dogs; one of them was a vicious Saint Bernard. The Saint Bernard, whose name was Turkey, was the most unfriendly and the most vicious of any my dogs. I knew in my mind that there was no dog around). The sound became louder, and by the time I opened my eyes, everybody was already looking in the direction of the growling sound. **"My goodness, a Christian brother was growling like a dog,"** I said to myself. Dogs do growl when they are afraid, and it is a warning to back off. The growling of a dog can be compared to the sound that comes from the tail of a rattlesnake. Failure to back off from the growl can result in a bite.

The growl coming from this brother got almost everyone praying louder than usual. I believe that some within the outreach team were scared, and others were in shock. Interestingly, we managed to bind those demons in the Name of Jesus, and everything became seemingly normal again. In retrospect we did not properly bind the demons. There is the right, partial, and wrong way to bind demons. An inexperienced Christian is likely to do a partial binding, which is not good, because the demons will be loosed again within a short period. That morning we did a partial binding, because later that night the growling came back about eight hours later. I was taking this brother and another Christian to their respective homes, when suddenly, the growling sound came again; he was alone in the back seat, and when I looked in the rear-view mirror, it appeared that he was coming for my throat, so I pulled to a stop and commanded the demons to leave. Some of the demons that manifested themselves included the spirit of anger, rejection, rebellion, homosexuality, and some lesser ranking demons. Some of these demons gained access to his mind while he was a little boy. This brother in the Lord was by no means possessed by these demons; a child of God cannot be possessed by demonic spirits, because the Holy Spirit dwells in the regenerated spirit of a believer; however, they can attack the body or the mind of a believer, and even gain access to the mind or body. I need to say that this brother with the demonic problem is now in the ministry and is doing a great job for the Lord, especially in the area of music, The mind is the territory where warfare rages between the flesh and the human spirit. But we must remember that God has made avenues for escape from demonic or any type of bondage: "And that they may recover themselves out of the snare of the devil, who are taken captive by him at his will" (**Second Timothy 2:26**) KJV.

I spoke to this brother who did growl 10 years after the initial growling episode, and he was still delivered. Thanks be to God for deliverance! Growling is not the only way that demons manifest, and all demons do not growl they all have different personalities, and they manifest themselves differently. Sometimes a person being prayed for may begin to speak in a different voice, and sometimes in tongues or language to confuse the inexperienced deliverance minister. In addition, demons also like to scream during church services. Unfortunately, some churches associate screaming as a sign of being "**touched**" by the Holy Spirit. Demons scream when they are excited to distract other worshippers or to attract unsuspecting worshippers to the one screaming. Moreover, some demons manifest by moving in snake-like fashion and some do hiss like a cat.

Chapter Three
The Demon Refused to Leave

"And when he was some into the house, his disciples asked him privately, why could not we cast him out? And he said unto them. This kind can come forth by noting, but by prayer and fasting" (**Mark 9:28,29**) KJV.

All of us can identify with this story. If you have a loved one who was in trouble either physically, emotionally, mentally, or spiritually. All of us are affected when our loved ones are going through, especially if the afflicted are children. It hurts me when I see starving and sick children on television or in any of my international travels. The father of the tormented boy felt powerless and perhaps felt like a failure because he was unable to help his son.

Have you ever felt like a failure? Perhaps, as a parent, something happened beyond your control. Perhaps in business ventures and for some reasons things took a nose-dive. One of the lessons in life is that there are some things beyond our control. Recently, Hurricane IAN came through Florida and destroyed homes, lives, and businesses. Sometimes as human beings we try to think about what could have been done differently and often find blame and ascribe it to someone, anyone, even God. We want to come up with an answer by asking why?

One of Job's friends blamed him for the terrible things that happened to him. Eliphaz believed that the calamities were the result of Job's wickedness.

"Then Eliphaz the Temanite answered and said, Can a man be profitable unto God, as he that is wise may be profitable unto himself? Is it any pleasure to the Almighty, that thou art righteous? or is it gain to him, that thou makest thy ways perfect? Will he reprove thee for fear of thee? will he enter with thee into judgment? Is not thy wickedness great? and thine iniquities infinite? For thou hast taken a pledge from thy brother for nought and stripped the naked of their clothing. Thou hast not given water to the weary to drink, and thou hast withholden bread from the hungry (**Job 22:1-7**) KJV.

Then Job, in ignorance, blames God in chapter twenty-three of the book of Job.

"Job said, Today I complain bitterly, because God has been cruel and made me suffer. If I knew where to find God, I would go there and argue my case. Then I would discover what he wanted to say. Would he overwhelm me with his greatness? No! He would listen because I am innocent, and he would say, "I now set you free!" I cannot find God anywhere— in front or back of me, to my left or my right. God is always at work, though I never see him. But he knows what I am doing, and when he tests me, I will be pure as gold. I have never refused to follow any of his commands, and I have always treasured his teachings. But he alone is God, and who can oppose him? God does as he pleases, and he will do exactly what he intends with me. Merely the thought of God All-Powerful makes me tremble with fear. God has covered me with darkness, but I refuse to be silent" (**Job 23:1-17**) Contemporary English Version.

Mark tells the event when the disciples of Christ were approached by a father whose son was tormented by demons. Jesus was not present for He was with Peter, James, and John on the mountain where He was transfigured. After His meeting with Elijah and Moses on the mountain, Jesus, Peter James and John descended to see a large crowd where the other nine disciples were gathered. Among the crowd were the Scribes who took advantage of Christ's absence to create a little commotion. Scribes in ancient Israel were distinguished professionals who exercised functions we would associate with lawyers, government ministers, judges, or even financiers, as early as the 11th century BCE. Some scribes copied documents, but this was not necessarily part of their job. Also among the crowd was a father in distress who spoke up.

"And one of the multitudes answered and said, Master, I have brought unto thee my son, which hath a dumb spirit; And wheresoever he taketh him, he teareth him: and he foameth, and gnasheth with his teeth, and pineth away: and I spake to thy disciples that they should cast him out; and they could not" (**Mark 9:17,18**) KJV.

It is noteworthy to mention that the disciples of Christ had already been given authority and power over demons to cast them out as recorded in Mathew and Luke; and they have actually exercised the authority and demons submitted themselves through the authority in the name of Jesus.

"And when he had called unto him his twelve disciples, he gave them power against unclean spirits, to cast them out, and to heal all manner of sickness and all manner of disease" (**Matthew 10:1**) KJV.

"And the seventy returned again with joy, saying, Lord, even the devils are subject unto us through thy name. And he said unto them, I beheld Satan as lightning fall from heaven. Behold, I give unto you power to tread on serpents and scorpions, and over all the power of the enemy: and nothing shall by any means hurt you" (**Luke 10:17-19**) KJV.

So, what hindered them from casting out demons from the tormented young man?

The story of the tormented young man is also illustrated in the gospel according to (**Matthew Chapter 17**)

The young man's condition is described as "**lunatic**" (**Matthew 17:15**). The word lunatic also translates into epileptic seizures or "**moonstruck**". Luna is the Latin word for moon. A "**moonstruck**" person is associated with psychosis in some cultures. At the time of Jesus, epilepsy was considered as a disgraceful disease and was supposed to have been inflicted on persons who had sinned against the moon. Some in our time calls it the "**devil's disease**" because there is no known cure. However, epileptic seizures can be managed with medications in most cases.

The lad's father believed that a demonic spirit is behind the torment of his son. "A spirit taketh him, and he suddenly crieth out: teareth him so that he foameth again and bruising him, hardly departeth from him" (**Luke 9:39**) KJV

In a similar manner, Mark quoted the lad's father saying to Jesus, "I have brought unto thee my son, who hath a dumb spirit: and wherever he taketh him, he teareth him: and he foameth, and gnasheth with his teeth, and pineth away" (**Mark 9:17,18**).

So far, we have gathered from the Word of God that the lad has more than one unclean demon, among which is a dumb spirit. Demons usually operate as a group, each helping one another for support, especially during exorcism. Demons not only work as a group but also have hierarchy. Some are more powerful that the others and the most powerful is usually referred to as the ruling spirit also known as the "strong man".

"But no one can, having entered into his house, plunder the goods of the strong man unless he first bind the strong man, and then he will plunder his house" (**Mark 3:27**) KJV

The ruling spirit in any group is usually the last and most difficult to cast out. Many deliverances have been performed without the expulsion of the ruling spirit: and in such cases the problems which brought about the deliverance sessions will reoccur, and often worsen. It does more harm than good whenever an inexperienced Christian attack demons to cast them out. Every believer has the authority to cast out demons, but not every believer qualifies to cast them out. There are dos and don'ts in every profession, and some mistakes can sometimes be fatal. For example, the surgical crew all know the "**dos and don'ts**" whenever an operation is to be performed, and you will never see a first-year resident perform brain surgery. Similarly, anyone who is interested in casting out demons should have an experienced person around or must himself be experienced. We need to learn from the mistakes of the seven sons of Sceva. "But one evil spirit retorted, Jesus I know, and Paul I know about: But who are you? Then the man in whom the evil spirit dwelt leaped upon them, mastering two of them, and was so violent against them that they dashed out of that house in fear stripped naked and wounded." (**Acts 19:15,16**) KJV

Casting out demons is not a game, demons are real, and some are more wicked than others. There was an incident during a shut-in service in which the ruling demon refused to leave. After praying for a young lady, I asked her to repeat the following after me: "**The Blood of Jesus sets me free.**" She did not. At first, I thought that she did not understand what I said because of my African accent; so, I decided to slowly repeat myself. When she did not say anything the second time, I knew that something was wrong, because she lowered her hands which were initially raised up, and on top of that she looked at me defiantly. Immediately, an attack was launched against the surfacing spirit. "**I rebuke you in 'the Name of Jesus Christ.**" She then staggered backwards. Then I said, "**I bind you by the Blood of Jesus Christ.**" This time she fell to the floor and was crawling away from me in a snake-like fashion. The first demon was a serpentine spirit, identified by slithering movement and the hissed like a cat. No sooner than this was cast out, another demon surfaced. She was more challenging this time, but the demon was also expelled. It was a four-legged demon, also identified by movement.

Finally, the ruling spirit surfaced; this time she was on her feet. She laughed mockingly and walked away from me in a confident gesture. I asked those present to keep repeating "the Blood of Jesus". She appeared to be getting weaker as time progressed. I was also getting a bit tired. It is not advisable to perform exorcism when tired; therefore, I decided to take another route. I threatened the demon, then commanded the ruling spirit to depart. It was the spirit of rebellion. He departed after a big jerk and the lady was as if dead. However, I did not realize that this client was under the influence of two ruling spirits until shortly after: a loud scream was heard and this time it was the spirit of lesbianism. I was in no physical condition to successfully launch a good attack on this demon. Besides, I did not have experienced people to help me on this occasion; my wife was also busy with another victim. The demon refused to leave, and unfortunately, we had to leave her alone.

There are several reasons why this lady was left undelivered. The first is obvious, I was at the time in no physical condition to cast this spirit out. Perhaps, my level of authority at the time was not sufficient. Although tired our strength in casting out demons does not lie in our physical ability but in Jesus. But in dealing with demons, their victims sometimes need to be restrained physically for their own protection. Demons do not care about hurting their host. For example. The spirit of suicide can influence the host during deliverance time to run against a speeding car. Physical restraint against an uncooperative person will get anyone tired. The second and perhaps the deciding factor was because she did not want to be delivered. A person's will plays an important role in a deliverance session; she was very uncooperative, and everyone knows God does not and will not force anyone against his will.

About six years after the above incident, a young man, whose family had been involved in Eastern religion, was possessed with many demons. This young man visited one of our Friday night services, the year was 1996. Suddenly, the demons began to manifest themselves through him. Ordinarily, his reactions could be classified as psychotic, but actually his actions were under the influence of demons. There are differences between the actions of a mentally ill person and one who is under demonic influence. There were times when he was hitting the pews with his fists, sometimes his face was twisted as a stroke victim, and words cannot describe his other physical movements. His deliverance took place within 8 minutes: however, within a couple of weeks, he went back into sin and became a slave to the devil again. There are people who want to be delivered, but do not want to pay the price to stay delivered. It costs to stay delivered and there are different levels of qualification necessary to force certain demons out. The disciples of Jesus **"asked him privately, why could not we cast him out?"** These disciples were surprised about their seeming failure for they had already been given power and authority to cast out demons. "And he calls the twelve to him; and he began to send them out two and two and gave to them power over the unclean spirits" (**Mark 6:7**) KJV; and prior to this incident, they had cast out some demons. I was able to identify with the disciples when they asked Jesus "why could not we cast him out?" "This Kind Can Come forth by Nothing, But by Prayer And Fasting" (**Mark 9:29**) KJV.

Let us examine the answer of Jesus to their question. What does He mean by **"this kind"**? First, this kind denotes a group or category. Demons always work together as a group, there is never any instance when a demon is alone without other demons present. Demons hate to be alone by themselves, and a demon can be frightened by the threat of isolation. In every group or category, a ruling spirit surrounds himself with lower ranking demons for support. In this case, the ruling spirit was the spirit of epilepsy. The medical profession believes that epilepsy is hereditary: some call it **"the devil's disease"** because of the inability of the victim to control himself during the seizures. It is said to be caused by either a brain injury or a disease in other organs reacting upon the brain. Some also told by the medical profession that there is no known cure for this disease. The reason for no medical cure is because it is the **"devil's disease"**; a demonic spirit is behind the problem, and the cure is in Jesus. The disciples of Jesus were faced with a ruling spirit that required special consecration. Fasting is essential when dealing with certain ruling spirits; prayers and fasting create a powerful force to drive out any ruling spirit.

Chapter Four
Who Let the Dogs Out?

"Look out for the dogs, look out for the evildoers, look out for those who mutilate the flesh" **Philippians 3:2** (English Standard Version)

There was a time that we had to call law enforcement because a dog in the neighborhood broke into our fence several times because one of our three female dogs was in heat. Peppy was a Great Dane that we raised from a puppy to an adult. At the time, we had a wooden fence but this intruder dog, a German Shepherd from the neighborhood, came more than once broke into our fence to "**befriend**" Peppy who was in heat. The two other dogs, Twinkle and Candy, barked to inform us of the arrival of the stranger, and we finally decided to find out where the intruder dog lived. Unfortunately, the dog was aggressive and did not allow us to approach the house as he demonstrated aggressive behavior. I did not want to be bitten; Therefore, we called the authority, and we showed the Police officer where the dog lived and when we arrived at the owner's house the intruder dog was not on leash and tried to bite the Police officer. The Police issued a citation, and we went to court to force the owner to have her dog on a leash or else. The Judge asked if we wanted to be compensated for the many times the intruder dog broke into our fence. We told the Judge no and that we only wanted the dog to be put on a leash.

Wild dogs have no master, have different personalities, and sometimes gather as a group. They roam freely in some countries. Some wild dogs are not aggressive at all, some are curious when people gather for picnics and hope to pick up some food. One thing wild dogs want is to survive by just looking for food wherever possible. In Honduras, I saw many wild dogs on the streets. Paul was issuing a warning about people that behave like wild dogs. The question is, who let the dogs out? Or who unleashed these wild dogs? The answers may surprise you.

Let's examine how the first dog was let out: Let us pay a visit to the Garden of Eden when a couple that we know as Adam and Eve were given the opportunity of a lifetime. God created Eve for Adam so the both of them could enjoy each other and reproduce others in the image of God. Everything was created for both of them, and God gave them dominion over everything that He created including the devil. There was no conflict; none of the animals had an appetite to kill and devour one another. They all enjoyed the season of innocence. Adam and Eve walked naked and were not ashamed. There were no predatorial animals. The wolf and the lambs dwelt together, cats and dogs did not chase each other. Tigers did not kill another animal for food. The leopards played with goats, the lions and cows were playmates, and the lions ate grass. In addition, snakes were like toys and went about their business. It was a time of innocence until they allowed a lower ran raking creature who was demoted for his rebellion persuaded Eve through deception to violate her creator. The leash was taken off; their eyes and every creature's eyes were opened and violence and killings began. One of the two young brothers took on a violent nature, an animalistic nature and killed his brother. Abel was the victim of his own brother Cain who was let loose through the rebellion of their parents. The animalistic nature of a wild dog was unleashed. Therefore, Cain lived in the Land of Nod, also translated as the land of "wandering." He was a "marked" man!

"And Cain went out from the presence of the LORD, and dwelt in the land of Nod, on the east of Eden" (**Genesis 6:16**) KJV

Cain was banished to the land of Nod or in the land of "**wandering**" because he committed the first capital offense. He was no longer allowed in Eden. There is a difference between dogs that live in the house and those that live on the streets. Turkey was the name of my Saint Bernard. He grew up in the streets and was adopted. Turkey was not a friendly dog and had no problem with biting anyone who came close to him. Turkey was blind in one eye and was also the most aggressive of my four-legged family members. One day, Turkey and I were walking. He was actually taking me for a walk and suddenly out of nowhere came three or four wild dogs that surrounded Turkey and I in an alley in the south Nashville area. I was concerned their presence felt like an ambush. Turkey was not concerned nor intimidated, but I was until Turkey took them on and sent them running with their tails tucked between their legs. Paul warned the churches in Galatia of those that behave like wild dogs.

"Look out for the dogs, look out for the evildoers, look out for those who mutilate the flesh" (**Philippians 3:2**) English Standard Version

The "**evildoers**" are those in the church that has a wild dog personality. The agenda of these Judaizers was not to worship but to create confusion. They came to reverse the doctrine of salvation by grace through faith.

Apostle Paul asked an important question to the Galatian churches. The same question can still be asked of backsliders of the 21st century who might have been infiltrated by the "**wild dogs**" in the church who teach false doctrines.

"Ye did run well; who did hinder you that ye should not obey the truth?" (**Galatians 5:7**) KJV

The hinderer is none other than Satan who opposes the truth of the gospel and employs wicked people to do his work even in the church. There are many tools that Satan employs to obstruct the work of God.

"Wherefore we would have come unto you, even I Paul, once and again; but Satan hindered us" (**First Thessalonians 2:18**) KJV

Satan was able to recruit Sanballat and Tobias to present opposition to the rebuilding of the temple. There will always be opposition to the work of the Lord for Satan is an adversary. Sometimes the attack comes through being mocked to discourage or cause frustration. Sometimes the attack may be through destruction of church property and even violence may be perpetrated on worshippers to scatter the flock.

"But it came to pass, that when Sanballat heard that we builded the wall, he was wroth, and took great indignation, and mocked the Jews. And he spake before his brethren and the army of Samaria, and said, What do these feeble Jews? Will they fortify themselves? Will they sacrifice? Will they make an end in a day? Will they revive the stones out of the heaps of the rubbish which are burned? Now, Tobiah the Ammonite was by him, and he said, Even that which they build, if a fox go up, he shall even break down their stone wall" (**Nehemiah 4:1-3**) KJV

People who act like the wild dogs and their cohorts will not be allowed into the Great and Holy City. This city was shown to the beloved disciple as part of the reward for accepting Christ as Lord and

Savior. The great city has twelve gates, with an angel at each gate. The city is square in shape and the side has three gates with the walls made of jasper and the twelve foundations are made of precious stones. The dogs and their cohorts cannot enter this holy city that is prepared only for the children of God.

"For without are dogs, and sorcerers, and whoremongers, and murderers, and idolaters, and whosoever loveth and maketh a lie" (**Revelation 22:15**) KJV.

Chapter Five
The Portals

"And I saw three unclean spirits like frogs come out of the mouth of the dragon, and out of the mouth of the beast, and out of the mouth of the false prophet. For they are the spirits of devils, working miracles, which go forth unto the kings of the earth and of the whole world, to gather them to the battle of that great day of God Almighty" (**Revelation 16:13,14**) KJV

The bible speaks a lot about portals or gates. "Porta" is the Latin word translated into gate or portal. One of the portals can be opened with words from the mouth. There are gates to the underworld or demonic world, also, there are gates of heaven that can be activated through the words from the mouth. Words that proceed from the mouth can be consequential in many ways. Jesus says:

"The words that I speak unto you, they are spirit, and they are life." (**John 6:63**) KJV

The beloved disciple saw the release of demonic spirits through the mouth of Satan, the Anti-Christ, and the False Prophet. This reminds us that the spirit of a word generates a positive or negative result. God has shown Israel that curses, or blessings can be generated from the mouth gate. The twelve tribes of Israel were divided into two. Six stood on Mount Ebal and issued curses, and the other six on Mount Gerizim to pronounce blessings.

"Thou art snared with the words of thy mouth, thou art taken with the words of thy mouth" (**Proverbs 6:2 KJV**)

"Death and life are in the power of the tongue: and they that love it shall eat the fruit thereof" (**Proverbs 18:21 KJV**)

Portals of revelation can be opened through teachings, preaching, and worship.

"Enter into his gates with thanksgiving, and into his courts with praise; be thankful unto him, and bless his name" (**Psalms 100:4 KJV**)

Dr. Luke informs of the imprisonment of Paul and Silas and how heaven's portal was opened as a result of the two prisoners dared to open their mouth to pray and praise God at the darkest hour.

"And at midnight Paul and Silas prayed and sang praises unto God: and the prisoners heard them. And suddenly there was a great earthquake, so that the foundations of the prison were shaken: and immediately all the doors were opened, and every one's bands were loosed" (**Acts 16:25,26**)

The prison doors were supernaturally unlocked, which was the result of the prayer and praise that came out of their mouths.

Similarly, occult practices such as soothsaying, magic, witchcraft, voodoo, omen reader, sorcery are also gateways to the underworld. Such practices are strictly forbidden by God.

"There must not be found among you anyone who makes his son or daughter pass through the fire, or a fortune-teller, soothsayer, omen reader, or sorcerer, or one who casts spells, or a medium, a spiritist, or one who calls up the dead. For whoever does these things is an abomination to Adonai, and because of these abominations Adonai your God is driving them out from before you" (**Deuteronomy 18:10-12 - Tree of Life Version**)

In addition, negative words from the mouth, negative words to the ears and negative exposures to the eyes can lead to positive or negative portals.

"The eye is the lamp of the body. Therefore, if your eye is good, your whole body will be full of light. But if your eye is bad, your body will be full of darkness. If therefore the light that is in you is darkness, how great is the darkness!" (**Matthew 6:22,23 - Tree of Life Version**)

Similarly, what your ears are exposed to can also be consequential.

"Take heed what you hear" is a direct warning from Christ. For example, words that came out from ten of the twelve leaders sent to Canaan resulted in fear among the Hebrews and heaven heard their fears and complaints. Therefore, a journey that was to last about two weeks took forty years to arrive in Canaan because the people reacted to what they heard.

"And your children shall wander in the wilderness forty years, and bear your whoredoms, until your carcasses be wasted in the wilderness. After the number of the days in which ye searched the land, even forty days, each day for a year, shall ye bear your iniquities, even forty years, and ye shall know my breach of promise. I the LORD have said, I will surely do it unto all this evil congregation, that are gathered together against me: in this wilderness they shall be consumed, and there they shall die. And the men, which Moses sent to search the land, who returned, and made all the congregation to murmur against him, by bringing up a slander upon the land, Even those men that did bring up the evil report upon the land, died by the plague before the LORD" (**Numbers 14:33-37 KJV**)

Forty is the number of trials or testing as is evidenced by the wilderness wandering for forty years. Also, the life of Moses reflects three distinct forty-year periods. The bible reveals that, he spent the first forty years in the royal palace of Egypt; the second forty years were spent in the desert with Jethro, his father-in-law and the third in the wilderness trying to get to the Promised Land. While in the wilderness, Moses spent forty days with God on two occasions, and Jesus was also in the wilderness for forty days being tempted by Satan after He had fasted. The disciples of Jesus did not fast while Christ was physically with them. But they were given the "Keys" to lock and unlock, bind, and loose things on earth. Therefore, the seventy reported joyfully that:

"Lord, even demons obey us when we use the power and authority of your name!" (**Luke 10:17 Good Word Translation**)

The name of the Lord is one of the "keys" in a Believers arsenal in spiritual warfare.

"And I will give unto thee the keys of the kingdom of heaven: and whatsoever thou shalt bind on earth shall be bound in heaven: and whatsoever thou shalt loose on earth shall be loosed in heaven" (**Matthew 16:19 KJV**)

"Verily I say unto you, Whatsoever ye shall bind on earth shall be bound in heaven: and whatsoever ye shall loose on earth shall be loosed in heaven." (**Matthew 18:18 KJV**)

These "keys" represent access to restrict demonic activities and access portals. The master key is Faith: not weak faith (**Romans 14**), not saving faith (**Ephesians 2:8**), not dead faith (**James 2:17**), not intellectual faith (**First Corinthian 2:5**) and not temporary faith (**Matthew 14:30**).

Temporary faith was demonstrated by Peter when he had faith to walk on water, then took his eyes off Jesus. Then he became fearful when he noticed the windy weather and his faith began to sink with him.

"And when the disciples saw him walking on the sea, they were troubled, saying, it is a spirit; and they cried out for fear. But straightway Jesus spoke unto them, saying, Be of good cheer; it is I; be not afraid.

And Peter answered him and said, Lord, if it be thou, bid me come unto thee on the water.

And he said, Come. And when Peter was come down out of the ship, he walked on the water, to go to Jesus.

But when he saw the wind boisterous, he was afraid; and beginning to sink, he cried, saying, Lord, save me.

And immediately Jesus stretched forth his hand, and caught him, and said unto him, O thou of little faith, wherefore didst thou doubt?" **(Matthew 14:26-31 KJV)**

The faith of Peter opened the portal for him to walk on the sea of Galilee. However, his faith dwindled when he focused on the sound of the stormy weather rather than on the Word of the Master of the sea who says, "**Come**". Peter needed to continue listening and hearing the word, "**Come**" in his head and in his heart to stay afloat. Apostle Paul tells us that, "faith cometh by hearing, and hearing by the word of God" (**Roman 10:17 KJV**). The word of faith is simply "**come.**" The invitation to come has been extended to each one and the invitation has no expiration date. You and I have been asked to step out of the boat which has limitations and to walk on the sea with Jesus with unlimited access. Now, faith has a companion "**key**" which is the unconditional love of God as expressed in Galatians 5:6. In addition, Paul wrote to the Corinthians that, "though I have all faith, so that I could remo.ve mountains, and have not charity, I am nothing" (**First Corinthians 13:2 KJV**).

For the portal of miracles to open, your faith in God and your desire to intimately love God should be the motive. A desire to experience the power of the Holy Spirit must be predicated on seeking to know the person of the Holy Spirit and surrender to Him. Paul experienced the power of the Holy Spirit on many levels because of his yearning to first intimately know Him.

"That I may know him, and the power of his resurrection, and the fellowship of his sufferings, being made conformable unto his death; If by any means I might attain unto the resurrection of the dead." (**Philippian 3:10,11 KJV**)

There are so many levels to knowing God. The height, width, and depth are immeasurable; even the disciples who walked with Him did not know all that was to know about Him.

"Who can measure the wealth and wisdom and knowledge of God? Who can understand his decisions or explain what he does?" (**Roman 11:33 Contemporary English Version**)

One of the disciples who walked closely with Christ did not know that Jesus was the Messiah until the portal of revelation was opened to Peter.

"Simon, son of Jonah, you are blessed! No human revealed this to you, but my Father in heaven revealed it to you. You are Peter, and I can guarantee that on this rock I will build my church. And the gates of hell will not overpower it" (**Matthew 16:17,18 Good Word Translation**)

There are three ways that the portals of hell can be opened knowingly or ignorantly. First, the gates or portals of hell can be activated through occult practices. Unfortunately, there are many people who do not understand that the underworld is very real and is parallel and intermingled with our world. The underworld is the kingdom of darkness with Satan as the ruler. God warned the Hebrews to stay away from any occult practices for their own safety.

"When you come to the land that the LORD your God is giving you, never learn the disgusting practices of those nations. You must never sacrifice your sons or daughters by burning them alive, practice black magic, be a fortuneteller, witch, or sorcerer, cast spells, ask ghosts or spirits for help, or consult the dead. Whoever does these things is disgusting to the LORD. The LORD your God is forcing these nations out of your way because of their disgusting practices." (**Deuteronomy 18:9-12 Good Word Translation**)

The second way to activate the portals of hell is to blaspheme against the Holy Spirit which is to deny the virgin birth.

"So, I can guarantee that people will be forgiven for any sin or cursing. However, cursing the Spirit will not be forgiven. Whoever speaks a word against the Son of Man will be forgiven. But whoever speaks against the Holy Spirit will not be forgiven in this world or the next." (**Matthew 12:31,32 Good Word Translation**)

To Blaspheme against the Holy Ghost is to simply deny the virgin birth of Christ. It is undeniable that Mary was a virgin and remained a virgin until after Jesus was born. It is also undeniable that Christ depended on the Ministry of the Holy Spirit during His Earthly Ministry and is also undeniable that the resurrection of Christ was made possible through the Power of the Holy Spirit. Therefore, to deny the involvement of the Holy Spirit is the ultimate sin that grieves the Holy Spirit (**Ephesians 4:30**). It is the "**sin unto death**" that will open the portals of hell on the individual.

The third way for the activation of the Gates of Hell is not sinful. It is supposed to happen to those who are truly seeking the face of God. It is actually a good thing but not a pleasant thing. When one decides to follow Christ and to surrender to the Person of the Holy Spirit makes the dark world to unleash hell in form of persecutions against the individual or community of people including the Church. The scriptures below will support activation of a hell portal, but one must fight the fight of faith.

"In every way we're troubled, but we aren't crushed by our troubles. We're frustrated, but we don't give up. We're persecuted, but we're not abandoned. We're captured, but we're not killed. We always carry around the death of Jesus in our bodies so that the life of Jesus is also shown in our bodies. While we are alive, we are constantly handed over to death for Jesus' sake so that the life of Jesus is also shown in our mortal nature" (**Second Corinthian 4:8-11 Good Word Translation**)

"God has given you the privilege not only to believe in Christ but also to suffer for him" (**Philippian 1:29 Good Word Translation**)

"You also know about the kind of persecutions and sufferings which happened to me in the cities of Antioch, Iconium, and Lystra. I endured those persecutions, and the Lord rescued me from all of them. Those who try to live a godly life because they believe in Christ Jesus will be persecuted." (**Second Timothy 3:11,12 Good Word Translation**)

"Don't be afraid of what you are going to suffer. The devil is going to throw some of you into prison so that you may be tested. Your suffering will go on for ten days. Be faithful until death, and I will give you the crown of life." (**Revelation 12:10 Good Word Translation**)

Chapter Six
Exposing the Serpentine Spirit

"And the LORD God said unto the woman, what is this that thou hast done? And the woman said, The serpent beguiled me, and I did eat." (**Genesis 3:13 KJV**)

The Hebrew word translated into "serpent" is "nâchâsh" which translates into snake. The Greek word used, "ophis", has a broader meaning. It also translates to snake, but figuratively means "a malicious person". Many years ago, a snake slithered into a small church facility in East Nashville, and just about everyone vacated the building almost immediately. Some worshippers never came back to the facility and the church later relocated to another site. I am unable to say what kind of snake it was because like most of the people in the building that heard the word "snake" along with some sounds of screaming, almost everyone ran toward the exit door including yours truly.

Snakes come in different sizes, colors, and speed. But they all can be identified by their slithering movements, but all are not venomous. Among the venomous snakes are the Gabon viper, Black Mamba, King Cobra, Rattle snakes, Death adder, the Boomslang snake, and the West African carpet viper, which is a small snake, but venomous. Puff Adder is also included in the list of venomous snakes. Then, there are the constrictor snakes such as Anaconda, Python, and Boa constrictors. These are large snakes that squeeze life out of their prey before swallowing them.

The bible does not specify the identity of the snake that interacted with Eve in the Garden of Eden. Who knows? It may have been a python or Anaconda or King Cobra. Regardless, it must be understood that the period that Satan spoke through the snake was the time of innocence. There was no poisonous snake, and none presented any harm to Adam and Eve. There was no crime, no hatred and Adam and Eve walked in the Garden without clothes. They were naked and did not think that they were naked. Also, in this period, there were no predators and snakes did not bite nor had the capacity to do harm. It was a friendly and peaceful time until Satan deceived Eve through the "old serpent".

"Now the serpent was more subtle than any beast of the field which the LORD God had made. And he said unto the woman, "Yea, hath God said, Ye shall not eat of every tree of the garden?" And the woman said unto the serpent, "We may eat of the fruit of the trees of the garden: But of the fruit of the tree which is in the midst of the garden, God hath said, Ye shall not eat of it, neither shall ye touch it, lest ye die." And the serpent said unto the woman, "Ye shall not surely die: For God doth know that in the day ye eat thereof, then your eyes shall be opened, and ye shall be as gods, knowing good and evil" (**Genesis 3:1-5 KJV**)

Some people have questioned how the communication of the snake with Eve took place. Others have also questioned Jonah being swallowed up by a fish and surviving for three days and three nights. Further, some wonder how Christ multiplied a sandwich to feed thousands. Indeed, a lot of things in the bible are not designed to make sense. The bible is not a book of logic. It does not make sense if we look at the snakes from the rational logical thinking knowing that snakes have no vocal cords. But the Earth was different then. It was the dispensation of innocence. Remember a donkey spoke with a human voice? How did it happen?

"And the LORD opened the mouth of the ass, and she said unto Balaam, what have I done unto thee, that thou hast smitten me these three times?" (**Numbers 22:28 KJV**)

In my travels, I have been privileged to witness many things that do not make sense including here in the USA, strange things have been seen. For example, while ministering to a lady at a shut-in service, a serpentine spirit manifested. This spirit was identified by the slithering movement of the lady that came up for prayer. The power of the Lord knocked her to the floor, and she slithered like a snake and hissed like a cat. Demonic spirits manifest themselves in several ways. Some manifest through high pitch screams during church services, some through coughing, tears, defiant looks, and some through the rolling backwards of the victim's eyes. Lustful demons' manifest sensual movements, either standing up or on the floor under the power of God. Spirits of anger manifest through fuming or angry looks, and the spirit of rebellion usually likes to stand for prayers with both hands around the waist. Serpentine spirits are also known as "**Leviathan**", or "**Old Serpent**". Isaiah prophesied that, "The Lord with his sore and great and strong sword shall punish Leviathan the piercing serpent, even Leviathan that crooked serpent" (**Isaiah 27:1 KJV**). This spirit is sometimes responsible for the persecution of Christians. That is why Jesus said, "Ye serpent, ye generations of vipers behold I send unto you prophets, and wise men, and scribes: and some of them ye shall kill and crucify: and some of them shall ye scourge in your synagogues and persecute them from city to city" (**Matthew 23:33,34 KJV**). The influence of the Serpentine spirits can also be seen in backbiters and character assassinators. Paul said that "Their throat is an open sepulcher: with their tongues they have used deceit; the poison of asps is under their lips." The basic operation of demons is through deception. That is, to present something harmful as harmless.

Our first introduction to the Serpentine spirit was in the Garden of Eden.

"Now the serpent was more subtle than any beast of the field which the Lord God hath made." (**Genesis 3:1 KJV**)

The serpent was the instrument used by the devil to bring about the fall of Adam and Eve, and hence the fallen nature inherited by all mankind. This is because Adam and Eve represented the entire human race; "For as in Adam all die" (**1 Corinthian 15.22**). The "**Old Serpent**" deceived Eve into disobeying the instruction and command from God: "And the serpent said unto the woman, Ye shall not surely die" (**Genesis 3:4 KJV**). The seed of doubt was planted by the serpent's appeal is to the desires of the flesh, "ye shall be as gods, knowing good and evil." (**Genesis 3:5 KJV**).

The flesh feeds on doubt, and as soon as the devil planted doubt by saying "Ye shall not die", it gave the flesh the need and opportunity to disobey God. Paul said, "For I know that in me (that is, in my flesh) dwelleth no good thing; for to will is present with me; but how to perform that which is gook I find not" (**Romans 7:18**). Temptations that appeal to the flesh are usually tempting, for "every man is tempted, when he is drawn away of his own lust and enticed" (**James 1:14**). God does not want His children to be ruled by the dictates of the flesh; therefore, Paul said, "Walk in the Spirit, and ye shall not fulfill the lust of the flesh. For the flesh lusteth against the spirit and the spirit against the flesh; and these are contrary one to the other. So that ye cannot do the things that ye would" (**Galatians 5:16,17 KJV**). The Serpentine spirit's tactical appeal was not just directed to the flesh, but also to the lust of the eyes. This was achieved by drawing Eve's attention to the trees in the garden.

"And when the woman saw that the tree was good for food, and that it was pleasant to the eyes, and a tree to be desired to make one wise, she took of the fruit thereof, and did eat, and gave also unto her husband with her; and he did eat" (**Genesis 3:6 KJV**)

Eve "saw that the fruit of the tree was good for food and pleasing to the eye, and also desirable for gaining wisdom." (**Genesis 3:6**)

The basic operation of the serpentine spirit or the "**Old serpent**" has not changed. It is through deception and seduction. Many men and women of God have been deceived and are still being deceived and seduced in fulfilment of the end time prophecy.

"Now the Spirit speaketh expressly, that in the latter times some shall depart from the faith, giving heed to seducing spirits, and doctrines of devils." (**First Timothy 4:1 KJV**)

For example, a Pastor in Tennessee says that the pandemic that has killed thousands around the world is a "hoax" and threatened to kick out members of his congregation if they showed up wearing protective masks.

Another well-known Pastor said that the tithe is no longer required and apologized for his previous teachings about tithing.

The serpentine spirit has been infiltrating the Church for quite some time. Consider what happened in the Churches of Galatia.

"I am shocked that you have so quickly turned from God, who chose you because of his wonderful kindness. You have believed another message, when there is really only one true message. But some people are causing you trouble and want to make you turn away from the good news about Christ. I pray that God will punish anyone who preaches anything different from our message to you! It doesn't matter if that person is one of us or an angel from heaven. I have said it before, and I will say it again. I hope God will punish anyone who preaches anything different from what you have already believed." **(Galatians 1:6-9 Contemporary English Translation)**

Chapter Seven
Indispensable God

"Without me ye can do nothing" (**John 15:5 KJV**)

"For in him we live, and move, and have our being" (**Acts 17:28 KJV**)

There are many things in life that are important but are not indispensable. For example, having a washing machine and dryer in an apartment or a house is a convenience but not indispensable. Also, there are things in life that are indispensable such as the air we breathe, food, and water. The word '**indispensable**' means a necessary thing or being. The necessities of life are relative to one's culture and geographical location. Having a pet in the house is not a necessity except for service dogs for those who have emotional or mental conditions. A service dog is trained to do many things such as provide a sense of calmness and are able to anticipate anxiety attacks and even fetch medication for their owner. Those of us who love our pets often ignore the fact that dogs like humans have a lifespan and their departure can create a lasting void.

I have owned many different dogs such as Great Dane, Shit-Zhu, German Shepherd, Saint Bernard, Mutts and other breeds from my childhood to adulthood. The passing of Ajax left a void upon his death in 2018. He was a mutt dog, part Shit-Zhu mixed with something else. Thinking back, he was stubborn as a goat from his life as a puppy till fully grown. He had his own mind and thought he had as much right to our house. When he was a puppy, he barked at the wind, airplanes, and anything to get attention. He was like our child. Then, he became sick and couldn't do anything for himself, he became weak, and I took him a couple of times to an emergency Vet in the middle of the night and finally he went to his eternal rest. We still have his leash, pictures, and cage. We then decided that having another dog would have been a good thing, but we are not ready and may never be ready for another one. Pets are not an indispensable part of our lives.

Prayer is a necessity, education is important, even if one inherits a lot of money. Education may not lead to being rich, but the knowledge acquired cannot be taken away. I also see faith as being necessary for worship and support. Faith means many things to different people. There are those who subscribe to academic or intellectual faith, Scientific, Political, or religious faith. Then under religious faith is Hindu faith, Muslim faith Buddha faith, Jewish faith, and Christian faith. Faith is the belief and trust in something bigger than oneself. Some have mistakenly associated their faith with what money, power, or influence can do for them. The Christian faith believes in the necessity of congregating in worship to evoke the presence of The Living God. The presence of the Christian God in Christian living and worship is indispensable.

"We should not stop gathering with other believers, as some of you are doing. Instead, we must continue to encourage each other even more as we see the day of the Lord coming." (**Hebrews 10:25 - Good Word Version**)

"I can guarantee again that if two of you agree on anything here on earth, my Father in heaven will accept it. Where two or three have come together in my name, I am there among them." (**Matthew 18:19, 20 - Good Word Version**)

The name and attributes assigned to the God of the Bible indicates the indispensability of the Christian God. There is no being compared to Him.

"I am God, and there is no other. I am God, and there's no one like me." (**Isaiah 46:9 - Good Word Translation**)

He is –"I AM THAT I AM" Adam Clarke in his commentary explains it as "I am who exists" (**Exodus 3:14**)

JEHOVAH, means that he is self-existent (**Psalms 83:18**)

"That men may know that thou, whose name alone is JEHOVAH, art the most high over all the earth." (**Psalm 83:18 KJV**)

OMNIPRESENT is the attribute of God that allows Him to be present everywhere even in troublesome times (**Psalm 139:7-12**)

"Can any hide himself in secret places that I shall not see him? saith the LORD. Do not, I fill heaven and earth? saith the LORD." (**Jeremiah 23:24 KJV**)

OMNISCIENT is the attribute of the Christian deity that He alone knows everything and everyone including the thoughts of men and how many hairs each has. This includes the past, present and the future.

"Before I formed thee in the belly, I knew thee; and before thou camest forth out of the womb I sanctified thee, and I ordained thee a prophet unto the nations." (**Jeremiah 1:5 KJV**)

"For whom he did foreknow, he also did predestinate to be conformed to the image of his Son, that he might be the firstborn among many brethren." (**Romans 8:29 KJV**)

OMNIPOTENT relates to the attribute of God as having absolute power and He is the all-powerful and sovereign. However, God limits Himself not to exercise His power over the human will.

"The Almighty—we cannot find him; he is great in power; justice and abundant righteousness he will not violate." (**Job 37:23 English Standard Version**)

ALPHA AND OMEGA , "Alpha and Omega are the first and last letters of the Greek alphabet, and a title of Christ and God in the Book of Revelation. This pair of letters is used as a Christian symbol,[1] and is often combined with the Cross". "I am Alpha and Omega, the beginning and the ending, saith the Lord, which is, and which was, and which is to come, the Almighty." (**Revelation 1:8**)

"I am the first and the last, and there is no God except me." (**Isaiah 44:6 Good Word Version**)

PROVIDER: (**Genesis 22:13.14**)

"To confess God as provider is to believe he cares for the life he creates. All of our clothing, food, home, family, and all else we have is a gift from God."

"But my God will supply all your need according to his riches in glory by Christ Jesus." (**Philippians 4:19 Webster Version**)

GOOD SHEPHERD: Associated with Christ's sacrifice on the cross.

"I am the good shepherd: the good shepherd giveth his life for the sheep" (**John 10:11 KJV**).

GREAT SHEPHERD: This title is associated with Christ's resurrection and in the mind of God Believers also resurrected with Him according to **Ephesians 2:6**.

"The God of peace brought the great shepherd of the sheep, our Lord Jesus, back to life through the blood of an eternal promise." (**Hebrews 13:20 Good Word Translation**)

CHIEF SHEPHERD: Associated with Christ's return for His Church and with rewards according to Revelation chapter twenty-two, verse twelve.

"And when the chief Shepherd shall appear, ye shall receive a crown of glory that fadeth not away." (**First Peter 5:4 KJV**)

HEALER: Jehovah Rapha is the name of the God of the bible who heals. His power to heal the wounded and sick sin soul cannot be overemphasized. He also heals diseases, mental illness, and all infirmities.

"He is the healer of the brokenhearted. He is the one who bandages their wounds." (**Psalm 147:3 Good Word Translation**)

"Heal me, O LORD, and I shall be healed; save me, and I shall be saved: for thou art my praise." (**Jeremiah 17:14 KJV**)

THE ALMIGHTY GOD (**Genesis 17:1**)

Omnipotent in Latin and El Shaddai in Hebrew is what translates into English as "**God Almighty**" or "**God the All Powerful One.**"

This name sets Him forth primarily as the strengthener, nourisher, and satisfier of His people.

MEDIATOR: The Ministry of Christ as the reconciler of the sinful man with the Holy God and thus becomes the intermediary of the New Covenant through His Blood.

"Jesus saith unto him, I am the way, the truth, and the life: no man cometh unto the Father, but by me." (**John 14:6**)

"For there is one God, and one mediator between God and men, the man Christ Jesus." (**First Timothy 2:5 KJV**)

"And to Jesus the mediator of the new covenant, and to the blood of sprinkling, that speaketh better things than that of Abel." (**Hebrews 12:24 KJV**)

SELF EXISTENT: This attribute uniquely sets God apart from anything and anyone visible or invisible. (**Genesis 2:4; 3:12,14; 21:33**)

"Where wast thou when I laid the foundations of the earth? declare if thou hast understanding. Who hath laid the measures thereof, if thou knowest? or who hath stretched the line upon it?" (**Job 38:4,5 KJV**)

"For by him were all things created, that are in heaven, and that are in earth, visible and invisible, whether they be thrones, or dominions, or principalities, or powers: all things were created by him, and for him; And he is before all things, and by him all things consist of." (**Colossians 1:16,17 KJV**)

HOLY: This attribute reveals who God is, and as His sons and daughters, we can all aspire to be like Him through surrender to the Holy Spirit.

"But as he which hath called you is holy, so be ye holy in all manner of conversation; Because it is written, Be ye holy; for I am holy." (**First Peter 1:15,16 KJV**)

Chapter Eight
How to Become a Terror to the Devil

"Behold, I give unto you power to tread on serpents and scorpions, and over all the power of the enemy: and nothing shall by any means hurt you." (**Luke 10:19**)

The Christian walk can be simple and at the same time as complicated as one chooses. It is a journey that includes valleys, mountains, stop signs and yield signs. There are also potholes on the road, and "**watch for falling rocks**" and "**deer crossings**" signs. Depending on the season of life, the road may be icy or wet from rain. There is however, "Rest stops" for those who want to stop and rest or take a bathroom break. Or you may be in a hurry and choose not to stop even though you are tired. Meanwhile, you are the driver of the vehicle and the control of how fast or slow is in your hands. The vehicle key is in your possession which represents authority. I used to take my dogs with me in the car regardless of the size of the dog or the car.

Turkey was a Saint Bernard breed. I found him at the dog pound, and I chose to adopt him out of all the other dogs. Perhaps because I felt sorry for him for, he could see in only one eye. I had no idea that Turkey eats like a rabbit and ate a whole lot. He was also a mean-spirited dog. He had broken his chains so many times to chase another dog, cat or anyone that came close to my doorstep. Finally, I went to the Hardware Store to secure the biggest and strongest chain to restrict Turkey from being loose because of his strength. As Turkey's owner my responsibility is to feed him and to keep people safe by placing a sign that clearly states, '**Watch Out for Dog**'.

I was the owner and had the authority and power to keep others safe. But one day, I was bitten by Turkey because I came towards him from his blind eye, the scar is still visible today. Mistakes do happen in life when we fail to observe the obvious. The bible tells us a lot about Satan. His names reflect who he was and who he has become and what he does. Somehow, we forget the rules of engagement. We also forget that he is an enemy on the loose and he is at war with Christians.

"For though we walk in the flesh, we do not war after the flesh: (For the weapons of our warfare are not carnal, but mighty through God to the pulling down of strong holds;) Casting down imaginations, and every high thing that exalteth itself against the knowledge of God, and bringing into captivity every thought to the obedience of Christ; And having in a readiness to revenge all disobedience, when your obedience is fulfilled." (**Second Corinthian 10:3-6 KJV**)

There are a few important points in these few verses:

1.   Christians are in a spiritual warfare.
2.   The warfare is not against human beings.
3.   The weapons for this warfare are not physical weapons.
4.   The weapons are superior to the enemy's weapons; "they are mighty before God for the overthrow and destruction of strongholds." These are areas in the believer's life that the enemy uses as access points.
5.   Imaginations are old ways that lead to nowhere.

To be able to overthrow and destroy the devil's strongholds, it is important to know the provisions of God which includes access to the Holy Spirit, the Word of God, angelic beings, as well as weapons. I must emphasize that these are strictly Believer's weapons, and to become a terror to the devil's kingdom, the necessary initial step is to be acquainted with God through His Word and through surrender to the Holy Spirit. It is important to understand that mere church affiliation or membership does not qualify one for this warfare, for the devil also has church affiliation.

The key to complete victorious living is a process and is continuous. The enemy does not give up and he probes to gain access through the strongholds that may still exist. However, Satan is afraid of any believer that seeks to be close to the Holy Spirit through the study and meditating on the Word and praying in the spirit. Praying in tongues strengthens the spirit of a believer, Apostle Jude writes, "Building up yourselves on your most holy faith, praying, in the Holy Ghost" (**Jude 20 KJV**).

Praying in Tongues is the Spirit-given ability to speak in another language supernaturally. A Christian who surrenders to the Holy Spirit will be strengthened with power and will have the ability to exemplify the Christian character also known as the "fruit of the Holy Spirit" listed in Galatians, Chapter Five. The fruit must be differentiated from the gifts of the Holy Spirit which is associated with service. Both the fruit and the gifts are important for the effective use of the weapons of our warfare. As we look at these weapons, let us keep in mind that they are very real, and very effective.

"Stand therefore, having your loins girt about with truth, and having on the breastplate of righteousness; And your feet shod with the preparation of the gospel of peace; Above all, taking the shield of faith, wherewith ye shall be able to quench all the fiery darts of the wicked.

And take the helmet of salvation, and the sword of the Spirit, which is the word of God: Praying always with all prayer and supplication in the Spirit and watching thereunto with all perseverance and supplication for all saints." (**Ephesians 6:14-18 KJV**)

The Sword of the Spirit / The Word of God

In Paul's letter to the Ephesians, he informs them that the Word of God is one of the weapons used for spiritual wars. This spiritual weapon is described to be "sharper than any two-edged sword" or is superior to other swords especially those used by the Roman Soldiers in those days.

There are some noticeable differences between the swords used by the Roman soldiers and the Believers sword of the spirit, which is the word of God. First, we know that one is for physical conflict, and the other is for spiritual conflict. Secondly, the physical sword can be used effectively in one's hand, the spiritual sword is effective when spoken with the mouth. Thirdly, the physical sword is held in a sheath that hung from the waist, but the sword of the spirit can be held in the Believer's heart but activated with the mouth.

"So return to me and change the way you think and act, or I will come to you quickly and wage war against them with the sword from my mouth" (Revelation 2:16) Good Word Translation.

"And out of his mouth goeth a sharp sword, that with it he should smite the nations: and he shall rule them with a rod of iron: and he treadeth the winepress of the fierceness and wrath of Almighty God." (**Revelation 19:15 KJV**)

The Word of God is effective when a Christian keeps it in his heart (**Psalm 119:11**) and allows it to become alive when spoken.

"But what saith it? The word is nigh thee, even in thy mouth, and in thy heart: that is, the word of faith, which we preach; That if thou shalt confess with thy mouth the Lord Jesus, and shalt believe in thine heart that God hath raised him from the dead, thou shalt be saved." (**Romans 10:8,9 KJV**)

Prophet Jeremiah also tells us some significant truths about the Word. He likens it to a fire and a hammer (**Jeremiah 23:29**).

Fire is symbolic of many things such as God's presence (**Exodus 3:2-4**), purification, God's wrath (**Deuteronomy 4:24; 9:3**), God the Son in judgment (**2Thessalonian1:8**), Passion for God (**Luke 3:16**). Hammer as seen in Jeremiah **23:29** is a metaphor for power and force that can bring about a change.

"And from the days of John the Baptist until now the kingdom of heaven suffereth violence, and the violent take it by force" (**Matthew 11:12 KJV**)

The Blood of Jesus:

"And they overcame him by the blood of the Lamb, and by the word of their testimony; and they loved not their lives unto the death" (**Revelation 12:11 KJV**)

To an intellectual mind, the idea of the Blood of Christ as a weapon and a shield may sound ridiculous; but then the event of Jonah in the fish, or the feeding of 5000 people with five loaves and two fishes all sound ridiculous to the logical mind. I guess the instruction given by God to Moses and Aaron, which led to the divine protection of all the Israelites first-born also sounded ridiculous.

"For I will pass through the land of Egypt this night and will smite all the firstborn in the land of Egypt, both man and beast; and against all the gods of Egypt I will execute judgment: I am the LORD. And the blood shall be to you for a token upon the houses where ye are and when I see the blood, I will pass over you, and the plague shall not be upon you to destroy you, when I smite the land of Egypt." (**Exodus 12:12,13 KJV**)

I have personally witnessed that the Blood of Christ works as a spiritual weapon when invoked. Reactions have been observed with victims of demonic attacks, when the instrument of deliverance say,

"**I come against you with the Blood of Jesus**." Demons tremble when a believer confidently says, "**the Blood of Jesus is against you.**" Believing that the Blood of Christ serves as both a shield and weapon is not enough. We must let it be our confession also.

"They won the victory over him because of the blood of the lamb and the word of their testimony. They didn't love their life so much that they refused to give it up." (**Revelation 12:11 Good Word Translation**)

The Helmet of Salvation

"Let God's saving power be like a helmet, and for a sword use God's message that comes from the Spirit" (**Ephesians 6:17 Contemporary English Version**)

This is strictly a defensive weapon that gives protection for the Believer's thought life. Each believer is responsible for wearing this helmet by verbally putting it on. Those who ride on motorcycles are aware of the importance of wearing their helmets because accidents do happen and unfortunately many have died as the result of negligence to wear their helmets. Similarly, this spiritual helmet provides protection from negative words such as can generate fear, doubt, and insecurity in a believer's life. These negative words come to the underworld primarily to weaken or destroy faith.

"And he said unto them, Take heed what ye hear: with what measure ye mete, it shall be measured to you: and unto you that hear shall more be given" (**Mark 4:24 KJV**).

What we hear is directly related to our faith or lack of faith. Be careful what you are hearing without the spiritual helmet. It has been said that "The measure of thought and study you give to the truth you hear will be the measure (of virtue and knowledge) that comes back to you, and more will be given to you who hear" (**Mark 4:24**). Also, since "faith cometh by hearing, and hearing by the word of God" (Roman 10:17), then we know that fear, doubts, and other negative words can come by hearing faithless words.

Putting on this "**Helmet of Salvation**" is every Believer's responsibility. Remember that demons are very good in making suggestions either directly into our thinking faculties, or using human beings, even Christians, to say unedifying words to our ears. It is suggested for every believer to daily say, "**Father, I cover both my**

thinking and my hearing faculties today with my Helmet of Salvation."

In addition to using the Helmet, Apostle Paul says that it is also important to be ready "to cast down imaginations and every high thing that exalteth itself against the knowledge of God and banging into captivity every thought to the obedience of Christ" (Second Corinthian 10:5 KJV).

The Shield of Faith

"Above all, taking the shield of faith, with which you shall be able to quench all the fiery darts for the wicked." (**Ephesians6:16, KJV**)

Notice the significance of these two words, "**above all**" which implies the importance of protecting faith through "shield or armor of faith" because the devil's attacks are directed at the faith of a believer. The importance of this shield cannot be overemphasized because it is through faith that we please God. Therefore, "**all the fiery darts**" that come from the devil are directed at the Christian's faith. God expects our faith to "stand" the enemy's attacks. Without your "**shield of faith**", you cannot successfully "**fight the good fight of faith**" (**1Timothy 6:12**).

The shield is available for everyone who wants to please God, wants to grow spiritually, and impact the lives of others. For example, the only recorded prayer of Jesus for Peter is for his faith to remain strong.

"And the Lord said, Simon, Simon, behold, Satan hath desired to have you, that he may sift you as wheat: But I have prayed for thee, that thy faith fail not: and when thou art converted, strengthen thy brethren" (**Luke 22:31,32, KJV**)

There are different factors that can cause one's faith to fail such as life's crises, sometimes due to seemingly unanswered prayers, or family crises, financial crises, or health crises. Many people's faith has been weakened or destroyed during the pandemic and some have either stopped attending church services or stopped giving to the church. What many young Christians fail to realize is that there are times when God allows some of the fiery darts to pass through so that the faith of a Believer could be tried. "Beloved, think it not strange concerning the fiery trial, which is to try you, as though some strange thing happened unto you" (**First Peter 4:12**).

There are reasons why God allows our faith to be tried. From the amplified Bible, Peter says "This proving of your faith is intended to rebound to (your) praise and glory and honor when Jesus Christ, the Messiah, the Anointed One, is revealed" (**First Peter 1:7**). Also, James says "Be assured and understand that the trial and proving of your faith brings out endurance and steadfastness and patience" (**James 1:3**).

It must be understood that trials bring out the best in the believer and name of Jesus is glorified!

"**What's in a Name?**" comes from Shakespeare's Romeo and Juliet. The truth to this phrase is Everything. Adolph Hitler is associated with Germany and the murder of about six million Jews. Donald Trump is associated with Trump Tower and the Presidency of the United States of America. Barak Obama is associated with the first African American to hold the office of the United States and under whose leadership the Al Qaeda leader Ben Laden was killed. Also, Vladmir Putin is associated with the leadership of Russia and who may be the instrument of WW3. Similarly, the name of Jesus is associated with the God-Man that sacrificed Himself for the sin of mankind in order to reconcile us with God. His name the bible tells us is "**above every name**"; therefore, demons are afraid when Believers call out the Name of Jesus, just as bank tellers become terrified when a would-be robber says, "**I have a gun**". As a Christian, you can say to demons, I have the Name of Jesus as my weapon and the result is the same, for demons become terrified. However, one must have affiliation with the person of Jesus for the Name to be effective.

"Then certain of the vagabond Jews, exorcists, took upon them to call over them which had evil spirits the name of the Lord Jesus, saying, "We adjure you by Jesus whom Paul preacheth. And there were seven sons of one Sceva, a Jew, and chief of the priests, which did so. And the evil spirit answered and said, Jesus I know, and Paul I know; but who are ye? And the man in whom the evil spirit was leaped on them, and overcame them, and prevailed against them, so that they fled out of that house naked and wounded. And this was known to all the Jews and Greeks also dwelling at Ephesus; and fear fell on them all, and the name of the Lord Jesus was magnified" (**Acts 19:13-17 KJV**).

67

The "**vagabond Jews**" did not have affiliation with Christ therefore were overpowered by the demons. In dealings with unclean spirits, there are times when you must repeat a command forcefully, for the demons to leave. In my dealings with my dogs, they responded quicker when I speak authoritatively. Never say, "Please leave in Jesus Name" when dealing with demons. They respond better to LOUD commands, even though they have perfect hearing. I have owned several dogs that have perfect hearing, but most of the time they respond quicker to a command said loudly and forcefully.

Another important point is to always call out the demon by name. A demon's name is known by the activities. If a person is partially a completely deaf because of a deaf spirit, then, one should say, "YOU DEAF SPIRIT, I COMMAND YOU TO COME OUT IN THE NAME OF JESUS CHRIST".

There are times when the result is partial deliverance. There may be several reasons, one being the demon came out after dividing itself and leaving behind a part of itself. Demons have been known to do this "**dividing tactics**".

There are also times when a person that comes for help want deliverance from the torment of the demons, but not from the habit that opened the door for demonic attack. For example, a person who has lung cancer of the lung due to smoking and who continues to smoke cannot be set free. The spirit of cancer has a legal right if lifestyle changes are not made.

Case in point, a woman came to the church that I am presently serving as pastor, crying for help. She was bound by many demons, including religious spirits.   It was revealed to me that she must denounce her involvement with the "**Star of David**" before she could be delivered. She became hysterical when I asked her to denounce it, saying "**I am not going to denounce my Star of David—don't take my Star of David from me**". Then she got up and ran out.

Similarly, Win Worley shared an incident concerning "**two witches**" who interrupted one of his deliverance services. He said in his book, Annihilating the Hosts of Hell that, "**During the message, they walked to the front of the church, turned toward the congregation and began pronouncing curses upon all present... A wave of prayer rolled from the believers as several men moved in** to physically remove them. **The two witches stiffened, stubbornly resisting removal with more than natural power. The confrontation was a standoff till one of the believers was alerted to the Star of David worn around the Warlock" neck. He jerked it form him and the satanic power was broken, causing him to fall to the floor in a heap.**"

Every weapon known to man has a name, regardless of whether it is a conventional or a nuclear weapon. The Superpowers have weapons with names such as B-29 bomber, Minuteman II and Minuteman III, Missiles, Intercontinental Ballistic Missiles, Medium-range SS-20s, Pershing, Antiballistic laser beams, and biological or nuclear weapons, to name a few. The name of each weapon is very important, especially when they are put into use. For example, the world still remembers the effect of the atomic bomb dropped into Hiroshima from a B-29 bomber in1945.

Similarly, so, the Christian's weapons also have names, but there is only one recognizable Name for the weapons to operate. In the natural, there are voice activated equipment or fingerprint activated equipment similarly spiritual weapons can only operate without affiliation with person of Jesus.

The Philistine should have surrendered when David said, "Thou comest to me with a sword, and with a spear, and with a shield; but I come to thee in the name of the Lord of hosts, the God of the armies of Israel, whom thou hast defiled" (**First Samuel 17: 45, KJV**). The Philistine was not defeated with the stone from the sling but was defeated because of the name of the Lord.

"And these signs shall follow them that believe; In my name shall they cast out devils; they shall speak with new tongues; They shall take up serpents; and if they drink any deadly thing, it shall not hurt them; they shall lay hands on the sick, and they shall recover" (**Mark 16:17,18, KJV**)

Speaking with "**new tongues**" is an important truth in deliverance. In addition, we must be able to have our "loins girt about with truth" (**Ephesians 6:14**).

In the Biblical times, the expression, having "**your loins girt**" or "**girting up the loins**" was a metaphor used for preparedness. This is because the girdle served several purposes. For example, "**when** men needed freedom to work or to run, they lift the hem of the tunic, tucked it into the girdle to gain greater freedom of movement". Ralph Gower also points out that "the girdle was also handy for the insertion of weapons of tools." The girdle is also used to support and hold babies when carried on the backs of the mothers. This tradition is very common among African women to support and hold babies which they carry on their backs. This action gives the mothers the needed opportunity to do other things with their hands. Thus, with this armor of truth as part of your warfare equipment, can bring you victorious living, because "the truth shall set you free."

African mothers as well as other mothers in western countries have embraced breast feeding their babies for several reasons including the health of the newborn. However, the Apostle Paul encourages the "breastplate of righteousness" as part of the warfare equipment.

"Stand therefore.... having on the breastplate of righteousness" (Ephesians 6:14 KJV).

This was a piece of armor used by the Roman Soldiers for protecting the breast or chest area. It can be likened to a bullet proof vest used for protecting the chest and breast areas which contain some of the vital organs, of the body such as the heart and lungs. The chest or breast area is considered the love area of the body.

Breast-feeding in Africa is considered as symbolic of a mother showing her love to her child. Also, it was recorded for edification, that the disciple "who Jesus loved" leaned on Christ's breast (Jn. 13:25;21:20).

Therefore, this armor protects the love of a believer from "waxing or growing cold"; remember that "faith worketh by love". The enemy attacks the faith of a believer by using their "trusted ones" to betray the trust, and therefore gets one paranoid and vulnerable position; afraid to love again. This has caused some believers to build walls around themselves, making it difficult for them to show their love to others, and for them to receive love from other believers. The Word of God says, "A brother offended is harder to be won than a strong city..." (Proverbs. 18:19 KJV). In order to prevent your love from growing cold, you need to request the breastplate of righteousness. Jesus prophesied that in the last days, "And the love of the great body off people will grow cold, because of the multiplied lawlessness and iniquity" (**Matthew 24:12 KJV**).

In addition to protecting the "**love area**" of one's life, the enemy wants to attack the believer's walk of faith, evangelical walk, and from walking in love. That is why Paul writes,

"And your feet shod with the preparation of the gospel of peace" (**Ephesians 6:15 KJV**).

When the feet are properly protected, the believer can:
1. Tread upon serpents and scorpions (Luke 10:19)
2. Spread the gospel to others (Romans 10:15)
3. Walk in love (Ephesians 5:2)
4. Run the race with patience (Hebrews 12:1)
5. Avoid hurting the feet against the stone (Psalms 91:12)
6. Tread and trample upon the lion and the adder (Psalms 91:13)
7. Walk with God like Noah, Enoch, and others (Genesis 5:22,24; 6:9)
8. Walk in the newness of life (Roman 6:4)
9. Walk honestly (Romans 13:13)
10. Walk by faith (Second Corinthians 5:7)
11. Walk in the spirit (Galatians 5:25)
12. Walk worthy of the vocation (Ephesians 4:1)
13. Walk honestly (First Thessalonian 4:12)
14. Walk as children of light (Ephesians 5:8)

The fourteen listed above should express that "**feet shod with the preparation of the gospel of peace**" is not only a defensive weapon, but also an offensive weapon. As an offensive weapon, "Thou shalt tread Upon the lion and adder; the young lion and the dragon shalt thou trample under feet" (**Psalm 91:13**). It is therefore important to appreciate the weapons and shields provided for believers as expressed in the epistle to the Ephesians.

As a shield, venomous snake bites can destroy a child of God figuratively speaking. It's unavoidable not to step upon snakes, and most human snakes will find a way of revenge. Therefore, failure to dress properly can destroy a family and a ministry. In addition to Paul's instructions to the Ephesians about "the whole armor of God" James also informs his readers how to put the devil on the run.

"Surrender to God! Resist the devil, and he will run from you" (**James 4:7, Contemporary English Translation**).

Of all the weapons at the Believers disposal, only this weapon is associated with putting the devil on the run. The Believer with the weapon of submission appears dangerous to the devil, thereby causing him (**the devil**) to flee. The new Lexicon Webster's Dictionary defines flee as "**to run from danger**". Before the devil will run away from a Believer, the Word of God says there are two things that must take place. First, the Believer whom the devil considers as dangerous surrenders to the Holy Spirit. This is the Believer who has ceased to offer resistance to the Word of God. Submission to the will of God was seen in Jesus when He said, "O my Father, if this cup may not pass away from me, except I drink it, thy will be done" (**Matthew 26:42**). Also, He said, "I seek not my own will, but the will of my Father which hath sent me" (**John 5:30**). David's prayer to God is also very relevant, "Teach me to do thy will; for thou art my God" (**Psalm 143:10**).

Equally important as to surrender to God is also the Believer who resists the devil's influence physically, mentally, and spiritually. You oppose him physically by not compromising the standard of holiness, you oppose him mentally by rejecting his thoughts, and you oppose him spiritually by using the "weapons of our warfare". Among the tools at Believers disposal is the power of prayer in dealing with the devil and his demons. Jesus responded to his disciples about their failure to cast demons out of a young man.

"And when he was come into the house, his disciples asked him privately, why could not we cast him out? And he said unto them, This kind can come forth by nothing, but by prayer and fasting" (**Mark 9:28,29 KJV**)

Prayer is perhaps the only weapon that everybody is familiar with, but often overlooked in spiritual warfare. Many people understand that prayer is our means of communicating with God, of requesting our needs from God, of asking for forgiveness, and giving thanks to God. But when it comes to dealing with demons, some Believers are simply ignorant.

One day, a brother came up for prayer, and his request was, **"please ask God to keep the devil from my back"**. Another brother said that he wanted prayer so that the devil could not find his home address. Prayer is not designed to keep the devil away. Another weapon is designed just for that. The weapon of submission or surrender is designed to keep the devil on the run, and even then, he only flees temporarily until another opportune time. Prayer can act as both a defensive and offensive weapon. As an armor, Jesus said "watch and pray, that ye enter not into temptation" (**Matthew 26:41**).

Prayer forms a hedge around a praying Christian. There are some things that God reveals through prayer, which otherwise would have been unknown. As an offensive weapon, prayer is the "**key**" for binding demonic spirits and loosening their victims. "And I will give thee the keys of the kingdom of heaven; and whatsoever thou shalt bind on earth shall be bound in heaven; and whatsoever thou shalt loose on earth shall be loosed in heaven" (**Matthew 16:19; 18:18**). Also, prayer and fasting work hand in hand when dealing with certain demonic spirits -"This kind can one forth by nothing, but by prayer and fasting" (**Mark 9:29 KJV**).

Chapter Nine
The Three Blood Sacrifices

"And almost all things are by the law purged with blood; and without shedding of blood is no remission" (**Hebrews 9:22, KJV**).

Once a year, rolling up my shirt sleeves for blood works has become a routine. It becomes frustrating when the nurses have problems finding the vein to draw my blood. Sometimes I will be asked to pump my fist a few times and sometimes asked to relax while the needle is going through my vein and then no blood comes out. I must admit that bloodwork is important for the recipient's physical well-being and to understand what sacrifice needs to be made to make life better physically. Blood tests also help determine if the organs are working properly and if the there is any disease in the blood. This body fluid called blood has many functions such as transporting oxygen and nutrients, preventing excess blood loss, regulating the temperature of the body and other critically important functions. It is therefore symbolic of life because excess blood loss can result in death.

In the bible, the death of an animal sacrificed, and collection of the blood is important under the Mosaic law. The animal must not have any defect because the animals sacrificed point to a larger sacrifice that was to take place centuries later at a place called Calgary. The of author of the book of Hebrews tells us that those who were defiled and unfit to worship in the Old Testament times were made clean through the sprinkling the blood of animals upon them. The significance of the exercise is to reveal a much better Blood that was to be shed centuries later.

"According to the Law of Moses, those people who become unclean are not fit to worship God. Yet they will be considered clean, if they are sprinkled with the blood of goats and bulls and with the ashes of a sacrificed calf" (**Hebrews 9:13, Contemporary English Version**).

The Holy Spirit wants us to know of the utmost value of Christ's blood in comparison to the animals sacrificed under the law. The point is that Christ's blood had to be shed for the redemption of the lost. **"Without the blood"** that was sacrificed by Christ Himself, all mankind would have been unfit to approach God.

"The blood of Christ, who had no defect, does even more. Through the eternal Spirit he offered himself to God and cleansed our consciences from the useless things we had done. Now we can serve the living God. Because Christ offered himself to God, he is able to bring a new promise from God. Through his death he paid the price to set people free from the sins they committed under the first promise. He did this so that those who are called can be guaranteed an inheritance that will last forever" (**Hebrews 9:14,15 God's Word Translation**).

It must be remembered that the animals sacrificed represented the defiled persons and had no choice in the matter. But Christ willingly sacrificed Himself by giving His Life so that we can have eternal Life.

"Because Christ offered himself to God, he is able to bring a new promise from God. Through his death he paid the price to set people free from the sins they committed under the first promise. He did this so that those who are called can be guaranteed an inheritance that will last forever" (**Hebrews 9:15 - God's Word Version**).

In addition, the shed blood of Christ provides opportunities such as:

1. Eternal Redemption (Heb 9:12; 1Peter 1:18,19)
2. Protection (Ex 12:13)
3. Sanctification (Heb 9:13; 1Pt 1:2)
4. Justification (Rom 5:8,9)
5. Cleansing (1Jn 1:7; Rev 1:5; 7:14)
6. To remove the stain of guilt on the conscience -Expiation (Guilt and sin) (Ish 59:1,2; Heb 9:22) Guilt is the stain of sin on the conscience
7. Peace between God and man (Col 1:20)
8. Because His blood calls for mercy and forgiveness (Heb 12:24)
9. To overcome (Rev 12:11)
10. Access to the Holy of Holies that only the High priest had access to under the Old Covenant (Hebrews 9:7; 10:19)
11. Boldness or liberty ("free confidence," grounded on the consciousness that our sins have been forgiven) to enter into the Holy

of holies because of the blood (Heb 10:19), for mercy and grace (Heb 4:16)

The devil also wants blood sacrifice for a different reason. His reasons are not for redemption but destruction, not to save lives, but to steal lives. His original desire to be like God has resulted in him trying in his quest to destroy everything and everyone that God loves.

He is thirsty for blood, he demands blood sacrifices, he enjoys it, and he encourages it by promising "more power" to those who perform the sacrifice. David says, "Yea, they sacrificed their sons and daughters unto devils, and shed innocent blood of their sons and daughter, who they sacrificed..." (**Psalms 106:37-38 King James Translation**.)

Dr. Rebecca Brown, a medical doctor who wrote He Came to Set the Captives Free informs us that, "in the United States there are eight 'holy days' out of each year when human sacrifices are performed." This is because the devil demands blood sacrifice for two reasons; First, blood sacrifice makes him feel important because he realizes that blood means life to God, and God is for life. Therefore, in order for the devil to feel important, that is, "to be like the Most High" (**Isa. 14:14**); he feels that by taking away a life (through the blood sacrifices to him), he is just as important as the God who gives the life.

Also, the devil wants blood sacrifices so as to desecrate the blood of Jesus Christ which was responsible for his defeat and for the redemption of many. In Dr. Rebecca Brown's book, a former Satan's high priestess gives an eye-witness account of a typical satanic human sacrifice. In the book, Elaine, the ex-high priestess says, "The main Easter sacrifice is always a man... In the eyes of Satan and the crown, that man becomes Jesus and Satan's supposed victory over Jesus at the cross is celebrated... The high priest urinated on the victim and member of the congregation threw feces at him while everybody cheered Satan's supposed victory and then bowed down and worshipped Satan... The victim's blood was drained off and mixed with drugs and alcohol and drank by the high priest and high priestess and passed through the crowd. Many of the crowd went up to desecrate the body. The night hours passed by while the drugged demonic frenzy of the crowd continued. Eventually the body was severed from the head and ground up, and portions mixed with drugs and other substances. Those who wanted more power are some of the mixtures." It must be understood that the devil is behind many murders, even mass murders. In my interview with Nashville's detective, Sergeant Mark Wynne, he told me of a man called Larry Hendrix, who murdered a five-month-old baby as a sacrifice to the devil.

"The police found pictures of him, and the baby taken at a cemetery. The baby was nude, and he (Hendrix) was holding the baby unlike in a sacrificial offering. We found music lyrics where he spoke of the power gained by the sacrifice of unbaptized souls..."

The influence of the devil is also seen in another murder, actually a mass murderer, called Adolf Hitler. Hitler was obsessed with the occult and the dabbled in demonic worship. To Hitler, the killing of thousands of Jews was a type of sacrifice to the devil. The devil **"was a murder from the beginning"** and to the devil the slaughter of Jews was type of revenge to the "woman which brought forth the man child..." (**Revelation 12:13**). The "**woman**" is Israel, and the "**man-child**" was Jesus.

In addition, the emblem of Hitler's Nazi, called a Swastika, can be seen with organizations that are involved in the occult, such as the "**skinheads**". In my interview, Nashville detective Sergeant Mark Wynne told me that, **"the skinheads are obsessed with the Nazi...and we have seen skin-head graffiti which is a Swastika and lightning bolt right along with occult graffiti. AS a matter of fact, we have investigated the individual... I can't give you their names, but we know they are in the skinheads and also involved in the occult worship..."**

The Nazi emblem is also called "**the broken cross**" is said to be ancient in origin. Each of the four equal arms for the cross is bent in a right-angle extension: "**Originally, it represented the four winds, for seasons, and four points on the compass... The Swastika shows the element of forces turning against nature and out of harmony.**" This Nazi emblem was also seen on the forehead of Charles Manson, the brain behind another gruesome mass killings of Sharon Tate and others such as Lino LaBianca and his wife, and Sharon's unborn baby.

The blood of his victims was used to write messages on the walls in 1969.

In Africa, blood sacrifice to the devil is usually done in exchange for wealth. It is a complicated process that involves the person who wants to be rich to volunteer as sacrifice to the devil the blood of the most important person to him without the knowledge of the potential sacrifice. The victim may be the man's wife, or first son, or the last son. The greedy cold-blooded criminal, if in polygamous practice cannot offer a wife that he dislikes. She must be a valuable wife to qualify for being sacrificed. The victim's blood can be taken supernaturally, and gradually, until the person dies for lack of sufficient blood. The victim also can be abducted and sacrificed to the devil. The mediator of this kind of contact is usually a special witchdoctor. This kind of hideous contract is not confined to West Africa.

The third kind of blood sacrifice is associated with the demands of those in power.

It appears that the needs of the people never seem important until the blood of the outspoken civil right workers is shed. For example, in 1955, Reverend George Lee's blood was shed for preaching about giving the black Americans the opportunity to vote in the State of Mississippi. Three months later, the blood of another civil rights worker was shed for organizing black voter in1955. Other blood sacrifices include that of three youngsters such as James Chaney, Andrew Goodman, and Michael Schwerner, who were sacrificed in one night by the Klan in 1964.

It was not until 1965 that the U.S. Congress passed the Voting Rights Act of 1965. It is not quite clear how much of the martyr's blood is required for those in power to respond to the people's needs. However, it is clear that without the sacrifice of blood, the people's needs are never met.

It is possible that those in governmental authority are trying to play God. If not, why was the first black police officer appointed the day following Medgar Evers funeral? And seven years later, why was Thurgood Marshall sworn in as the first black Supreme Court Justice?

Did the blood of Evers and others before him satisfy the blood requirement? Perhaps not, for in 1968 the assassin's bullet shed yet another blood, the blood of Dr. Marin Luther King. His blood was perhaps the ultimate sacrifice to those who are playing God. The shedding of his blood had allowed the people of color to be elected to mayoral offices, Gubernatorial offices, and also to the White House.

It also seems to me that all blood of the innocent shed in South Africa has satisfied the apartheid system. Because Mr. Nelson Mandela was released from prison and later became the president of South Africa. Glory be to God!

Chapter Ten
The Three Kinds of Hell

"Therefore, hell hath enlarged herself, and opened her mouth without measure…" (**Isaiah 5:14**)

I heard a man say, "**Go to hell**" in anger. The response from his wife is, "**I am already living in hell from the day you started drinking ten years ago**" The word "**hell**" means different things to people around the world. Those in war torn countries can tell you that they have experienced hell and are experiencing hell. An abused wife will say the same thing. Also, those living in bondage will confess the same thing. There are different kinds of bondages or oppressive situations that can be likened to living in hell for some. There are those living in hell because of political bondage, religious bondage, military bondage, cultural bondage, and social bondage.

For example, Sharia law is an oppressive religious law to keep women in subjection. Women must be masked in public, not because of covid-19 for this law precedes the pandemic. In addition, women are not allowed to witness a crime only men can testify when a crime is committed. Unfortunately, women are usually the victims of crimes. Also, under this law, it is a crime to abandon the Islamic faith. "**One of the hallmarks of Sharia law is the inferiority to which it classifies women. A common example is if a woman is raped and becomes pregnant, she is sentenced to death by stoning strictly for becoming pregnant out of wedlock. The man who raped her, however, is usually free of any wrongdoing**". Also, in military bondage. Martial law is imposed. Which is a "**direct military control of normal civil functions or suspension of civil law by a government, especially in response to an emergency where civil forces are overwhelmed, or in an occupied territory**" Russia recently imposed martial law in regions of the country of Ukraine.

"**Typically, the imposition of martial law accompanies curfews; the suspension of civil law, civil rights, and habeas corpus; and the application or extension of military law or military justice to civilians. Civilians defying martial law may be subjected to military tribunal (court-martial)**".

The point is there, can be hell on earth in countries where martial law has been instituted and where women are considered as less than men. Dr. Fatima Mernissi in her book, **"Beyond the Veil"** addresses the psychological impact of polygamy on both a male and a female, **"It enhances men's perception of themselves as primarily sexual beings and emphasizes the sexual nature of the conjugal unit. Moreover, polygamy is a way for the man to humiliate the woman as a sexual being; it expresses her inability to satisfy him"** Therefore, there are women around the world who are being subjected to hell on earth through humiliation.

Is There a Real Hell?

Years ago, in my teenage years, I blocked the fact that Hell exists out of my mind. I have always known that Hell existed but did not know whether its location was above or beneath. Also, the fact that I could end up I Hell while in my sin was frightening, so I pretended that it was not for me. I found out that most people who are living a sinful life do not like to think about Hell either. It appears to me that those who profess to attend a church and who are not living according to the bible might end up in hell. Even some of the Gospel preachers avoid the Hell-related preaching and may themselves end up in this place of eternal torment called hell. One brother said that **"the quickest way to turn people off is to preach about Hell."** Another preacher said that he stopped preaching about Hell, because his Congregation does not **"enjoy that kind of preaching..."** He said that the Chairman of his Deacon Board, with some of his Congregation, blamed the decrease in Tithes and Offerings on his last message about Hell. A visiting Evangelist said to the host pastor, **"You don't have to worry about me running off your members, because I only preach reality, and Hell is not real."** My recent thoughts about Hell were out of concern for those who are without Jesus Christ in their lives. And, for those who might be in backslidden condition. One of the truths that we know about Hell is that it exists. Jesus spoke of Hell as the place of final punishment.

Observation of the Bible verses about Hell give us an insight to its location. Words such as **"descend"** in Isaiah 5:14 and **"beneath"** in Isaiah 14:9 seem to point in the downward direction. Is it possible that

Hell is actually under the Earth that we live? And is it possible that the molten magma from a volcano is a sample of Gehenna-Hell in action? For a fact, we know that God and the devil cannot co-habitat; we also know that the devil is always to the opposite of the things of God; we also know that "**God is Light,**" and the devil represents darkness. Since we know that Jesus ascended into heaven, then Hell must be in the opposite direction, which is beneath the Earth. We also know that soon "the Lord Himself shall descend from heaven with a shout..." (**First Thessalonian 4:16**), and Christians everywhere will ascend "**to meet the Lord in the air...**" If you are not sure which direction you will go, will you please ask God to come into your life? Please say this prayer, so as to have the assurance of Heaven:

"LORD JESUS, I AM A SINNER.

LORD JESUS, PLEASE FORGIVE ME FOR MY SINS. LORD JESUS, I ACCEPT YOU AS MY LORD AND SAVIOUR. PLESE SAVE ME".

Finally, say, "JESUS, I THANK YOU FOR ACCEPTING ME AS YOU CHILD. FOR THIS IS THE BEST DAY OF MY LIFE, AND THE BEST THING THAT EVER HAPPENED TO ME"

Now, you are no longer hell-bound because you are a child of God. Going to hell should not be a concern to those who have submitted their lives to the Lordship of Christ. In the bible, there are three Greek words that are translated into the English word Hell. First is the Greek word Hades, which translates into Hell and which Strong's Exhaustive Concordance defines as "**the place (state) of the departed souls.**" This is the location of torment for those who have been disobedient to the will of God. Jesus gave an example of two people of different lifestyles on earth. One ends up in a good place and the other in a place of torment.

"There was a certain rich man, which was clothed in purple and fine linen, and fared sumptuously every day: And there was a certain beggar named Lazarus, which was laid at his gate, full of sores, And desiring to be fed with the crumbs which fell from the rich man's table: moreover, the dogs came and licked his sores. And it came to pass, that the beggar died, and was carried by the angels into Abraham's bosom: the rich man also died and was buried; And in hell he lift up his eyes, being in torments, and seeth Abraham afar off, and Lazarus in his bosom. And he cried and said, Father Abraham, have mercy on me, and send Lazarus, that he may dip the tip of his finger in water, and cool my tongue; for I am tormented in this flame. But Abraham said, Son, remember that thou in thy lifetime receivedst thy good things, and likewise Lazarus evil things: but now he is comforted, and thou art tormented. And beside all this, between us and you there is a great gulf fixed: so that they which would pass from hence to you cannot; neither can they pass to us, that would come from thence" (**Luke 16:19-26 KJV**)

Another kind of Hell mentioned in the New Testament Bible comes from the Greek word Tartarus, which was never designed by God for humans. This was designed specifically for the confinement of Fallen Angeles. The Greek word Tartarus is used only once in the Bible, when Peter writes that, "God spared not he Angels that sinned, but cast them down to Hell (**Tartarus**), and delivered into chains of darkness, to be reserved unto judgment (**Second Peter 2:4**). These fallen angels are still in confinement and "reserved unto judgment". Jude also writes that, "the angels which kept not their first estate, but left their own habitation, he hath reserved in everlasting chains under darkness unto the judgment of the great day" (**Jude 6**).

Many believe that the angels in confinement crossed the line twice. First, they crossed the line when they joined in Satan's rebellion. But also crossed the line when some of these fallen angels impregnated humans and their union produced a race of giants.

"The children of the supernatural beings who had married these women became famous heroes and warriors. They were called Nephilim and lived on the earth at that time and even later" (**Genesis 6:4**) Contemporary English Version.

One of the giants had six fingers on each hand and six toes on each foot.

"And there was again war at Gath, where there was a man of great stature, who had six fingers on each hand, and six toes on each foot, twenty-four in number, and he also was descended from the giants" (**Second Samuel 21:20**) English Standard Version.

The third Greek word translated into Hell is Gehenna, and is the only Hell associated with fire and brimstone. It is interesting to note that Gehenna-Hell is capable of enlarging itself; "Therefore hell hath enlarged herself, and opened her mouth without measure: and their glory, and their multitude, and their pomp, and he that rejoiceth, shall descend into it" (**Isaiah 5:14**),

Chapter Eleven
Deliverance

"For we would not, brethren, have you ignorant of our trouble which came to us in Asia, that we were pressed out of measure, above strength, insomuch that we despaired even of life: But we had the sentence of death in ourselves, that we should not trust in ourselves, but in God which raiseth the dead: Who delivered us from so great a death, and doth deliver: in whom we trust that he will yet deliver us" **(Second Corinthians 1:8-10 KJV)**

The term deliverance means different things to different people in different parts of the world. The word **"deliver"** is derived from two words, "de", which means "from" and "**liberare**" which means "to free". The dictionary defines the word "deliver" as, to set free or save from evil, danger etc. To the homeless man who finally found a place to lay his head without the threats of winter cold or extreme summer heat is deliverance from the agony of homelessness. To the jobless father who could not provide for his family and suddenly finds a good paying job to sustain his family is deliverance from shame and humiliation.

To the one who has been incarcerated, but later released on parole for good behavior is deliverance from the limitations of the prison system. To the mentally or physically abused spouse, deliverance means the stoppage of both mental and physical abuse. The biblical approach to deliverance is not different, but broader than the aforementioned. Some of the bible characters also suffered abuse, homelessness, imprisonment, and poverty, but in addition, the bible addresses deliverance from spiritual death, demonic oppression and even from financial bondage.

Webster's dictionary defines deliverance as **"to rescue from bondage or danger."** The scriptural meaning is basically the same as in Webster's dictionary. However, Paul in Second Corinthians chapter one verse ten uses three tenses for the word deliver. The scripture says, God **"who delivered us from so great a death and does deliver us; in whom we trust that He will still deliver us."** Paul expresses the accomplished work, present work, and future work of Christ in every believer. First, let's look at the accomplished work of Christ in the portion of the scripture of Second Corinthians chapter one verse ten. First, the reference to deliverance "**from so great a death**.". is both the physical and spiritual death. The deliverance of Paul from physical death is probably a reference to when he was stoned and left for dead at a place called Lystra "And there came thither certain Jews from Antioch and Iconium, who persuaded the people, and, having stoned Paul, drew him out of the city, supposing he had been dead. Howbeit, as the disciples stood round about him, he rose up, and came into the city: and the next day he departed with Barnabas to Derbe" (**Acts 14:19,20 KJV**). Paul was left for dead, but God delivered Paul by first taking him to the "third heaven" where he "heard inexpressible words, which it is not lawful for a man to utter" (**Second Corinthians 12:2-4**).

There are also many Missionaries around the world who have escaped death in one form or another. Also, many other people like myself that have survived automobile accidents and armed robbers. There is also deliverance from another kind of death from which every Christian has been delivered and that is spiritual death. This spiritual death was inherited by mankind from Adam and Eve because of their disobedience in the Garden of Eden. Every individual who accepts Christ and His atoning work on the Cross becomes instantaneously delivered from the spiritual death. Paul refers to the spiritual death as a result of sin in Romans 6:23. Spiritual death is a term used to describe separation from the Life of God. This separation from the Life of God is evident in the Book of Genesis, chapter three. This chapter introduces another character into the scene who was the avenue of spiritual death. We see a serpent who could talk and communicate effectively with Eve; but this serpent was no ordinary serpent. He is known by various names and titles such as "**Red dragon, Devil, or Satan**" and the list goes on. This enemy of mankind made a masterful presentation to entice Eve to eat the fruit forbidden for consumption by God. "And the Lord God commanded the man, saying, of every tree of the garden you may freely eat; but of the tree of the knowledge of good and evil you shall not eat, for in the day that you eat of it you shall die" (**Genesis 2:16,17 KJV**). The serpent made a very masterful presentation and today his masterful presentations of presenting harmful and dangerous things as harmless are still bringing many into bondage. His masterful presentations are evident on the internet, television shows, pornographic magazines, and telemarketing advertisements. It is a known fact that many of our young people have been seduced and trapped into pornography through the internet and some television shows. Also, telemarketers have also seduced many into the bondage of debt. Many young marriages have been weakened and even destroyed because of financial difficulties. According to the book of Proverbs chapter twenty-two, verse seven where it is stated that, large amount of debt is a bondage because "**the borrower is the slave to the lende**r".

There are different ways that God uses to deliver a person from any kind of bondage, or a nation from the oppression of another more powerful country. God can deliver instantaneously, progressively and in other ways that will be discussed in this chapter.

Webster's dictionary defines instantaneous as something that happens in an instant. As much as I enjoy the aroma of brewing coffee, and sometimes it's percolating sound. There is no substitute, in my opinion, for instant coffee. A boiling water, a cup, and ready-to-go coffee is all that is needed. However, the choice of instant or brewed coffee was not always mine to choose, especially if I was a guest in a house with no instant coffee.

There are many examples of individuals in the scriptures that experienced instantaneous deliverance. Among the recipients of instantaneous deliverance was a woman who had suffered from blood disease for twelve years. During these twelve years, she had made several attempts to be healed through the Physicians to no avail. "a woman having an issue of blood twelve years which had spent all her living upon Physicians, neither could be healed of any" (**Luke 8:43 KJV**).

Medical cost in the days of Jesus were relatively expensive as they are in this generation. As a result, the woman spent all her money on medical expenses. Medical expenses can sometimes be staggering and can easily wipe out life's savings, especially for those without adequate medical coverage. It is important to remember that medical knowledge would not be possible without God, and God sometimes chooses to heal through medical means, and sometimes supernaturally. The woman in question, had a kind of blood disease that was unknown to the Physicians of her time. Things would have been different if she was living in this twenty-first century with much more advanced knowledge. Dr. Luke tells us that her deliverance from the issue of blood was instantaneous. "A woman who had been suffering from chronic bleeding for twelve years was in the crowd. No one could cure her. She came up behind Jesus, touched the edge of his clothes, and her bleeding stopped at once" (**Luke 8:43,44**) God's Word Translation.

We also see another example of instantaneous deliverance through Apostle Peter:

"When Peter was going around to all of God's people, he came to those who lived in the city of Lydda. In Lydda Peter found a man named Aeneas who was paralyzed and confined to a cot for eight years. **Act 9:34** Peter said to him, "Aeneas, Jesus Christ makes you well. Get up and pick up your cot." Aeneas immediately got up. Everyone who lived in the city of Lydda and the coastal region of Sharon saw what had happened to Aeneas and turned to the Lord in faith" (**Acts 9:32-35**) God's word Translation.

Secondly, we see that God also delivers progressively as He chooses. For example, God said to Moses concerning the enemies of the Hebrews:

"And I will send hornets before thee, which shall drive out the Hivite, the Canaanite, and the Hittite, from before thee. I will not drive them out from before thee in one year; lest the land become desolate, and the beast of the field multiply against thee. By little and little I will drive them out from before thee, until thou be increased, and inherit the land" (**Exodus 23:28-30KJV**).

Here we see the Lord of Host with a promise to give victory to Israel over the Hivites, the Canaanites and the Hittites. He also told them the battle plan, "I will cause confusion among all the people to whom you come and will make all your enemies turn their backs to you. And I will send hornets before you, which shall drive out the Hivite, the Canaanite and the Hittite from before you" (**Exodus 23:27,28**) However, He states that the victory was to be progressive. The reason for this progressive deliverance is clearly stated, "lest the land become desolate and the beasts of the field become too numerous for you" (**Exodus 23:29**). In other words, the Israelites were not numerous enough to occupy and maintain the land immediately. The inability of Israel to immediately occupy the land will result in occupation of the unoccupied places by the wild beasts.

The application of this to our generation is to consider a sixteen-year-old who wants to own a car and has been taught to drive, however, he is not ready to own a car for a number of reasons such as, his or her irresponsible behavior. For example, he may not be responsible enough to lock the car at the Mall's parking lot or take care of the engine by putting oil in when the oil indicator light reads low, or perhaps he does not have a job in order to pay the insurance which is high for drivers of his age group. Therefore, his parents may decide to wait until he is a little more responsible, which perhaps will come with experience as he increases in age and excels in school. Eventually, the parents will allow their son to possess a car as he gradually matures and moves into a more responsible posture.

In addition to instantaneous and progressive deliverance is what I call partial deliverance. The example from the son of King Solomon, Rehoboam who changed from following the Lord when he felt that he had arrived. As a result, God sent an instrument of divine correction of Egypt named Shishak. The invasion of Shishak upon Jerusalem led to repentance and God gave partial deliverance to Rehoboam as a result of cockiness.

"And it came to pass, when Rehoboam had established the kingdom, and had strengthened himself, he forsook the law of the LORD, and all Israel with him. And it came to pass, that in the fifth year of king Rehoboam Shishak king of Egypt came up against Jerusalem, because they had transgressed against the LORD, With twelve hundred chariots, and threescore thousand horsemen: and the people were without number that came with him out of Egypt; the Lubims, the Sukkiims, and the Ethiopians. And he took the fenced cities which pertained to Judah and came to Jerusalem. Then came Shemaiah the prophet to Rehoboam, and to the princes of Judah, that were gathered together to Jerusalem because of Shishak, and said unto them, Thus saith the LORD, Ye have forsaken me, and therefore have I also left you in the hand of Shishak.

"Whereupon the princes of Israel and the king humbled themselves; and they said, The LORD is righteous. And when the LORD saw that they humbled themselves, the word of the LORD came to Shemaiah, saying, They have humbled themselves; therefore, I will not destroy them, but I will grant them some deliverance; and my wrath shall not be poured out upon Jerusalem by the hand of Shishak"(**Second Chronicles 12:1-7 KJV**).

Also, in the book of Judges, we find out that the tribe of Judah were successful through the help of God in defeating the Mountaintop enemies but were not successful with the enemies that lived in the valleys. They had partial deliverance because God wanted to test them.

"And the LORD was with Judah; and he drave out the inhabitants of the mountain; but could not drive out the inhabitants of the valley, because they had chariots of iron" (**Judges 1:19KJV**).

"Now these are the nations which the LORD left, to prove Israel by them, even as many of Israel as had not known all the wars of Canaan; Only that the generations of the children of Israel might know, to teach them war, at the least such as before knew nothing thereof; Namely, five lords of the Philistines, and all the Canaanites, and the Sidonians, and the Hivites that dwelt in mount Lebanon, from mount Baalhermon unto the entering in of Hamath. And they were to prove Israel by them, to know whether they would hearken unto the commandments of the LORD, which he commanded their fathers by the hand of Moses" (**Judges 3:1-4 KJV**).

Moses had to intercede for Miriam, his older sister because she became a leper for criticizing Moses for marrying an African woman. This led to a meeting called by God in which God was angry because of an unnecessary criticism of Moses by Aaron and Miriam. At the end of the meeting, Miriam became leprous. Moses pleaded with God and God responded by saying that Miriam's healing will be delayed learning from her mistake.

"And the anger of the LORD was kindled against them; and he departed. And the cloud departed from off the tabernacle; and behold, Miriam became leprous, white as snow: and Aaron looked upon Miriam, and behold, she was leprous. And Aaron said unto Moses, Alas, my lord, I beseech thee, lay not the sin upon us, wherein we have done foolishly, and wherein we have sinned. Let her not be as one dead, of whom the flesh is half consumed when he cometh out of his mother's womb. And Moses cried unto the LORD, saying, Heal her now, O God, I beseech thee.

And the LORD said unto Moses, If her father had but spit in her face, should she not be ashamed for seven days? let her be shut out from the camp seven days, and after that let her be received in again" (**Numbers 12:9-14 KJV**).

Chapter Twelve
Deception

"And no wonder, for even Satan disguises himself as an angel of light" (**Second Corinthians 11:14**) English Standard Version.

False presentation of self or of a product is the root behind deception. The "**Old**" serpent presented himself as a friend of Eve to get her to eat of the forbidden fruit. First, the conversation started with a question about what God said to Adam about the forbidden fruit. Then, he created a doubt in Eve's mind about what God told Adam.

"The snake was sneakier than any of the other wild animals that the LORD God had made. One day it came to the woman and asked, "Did God tell you not to eat fruit from any tree in the garden?" (**Genesis 3:1**) Contemporary English Version

The force behind the snake is Satan himself who pretended to be ignorant of God's instructions to Adam, and convinced Eve that death will not happen.

In fact, both physical and spiritual death happened to Adam and Eve and extended to all mankind.

"For as in Adam all die, even so in Christ shall all be made alive" (**First Corinthians 15:22 KJV**)

Many still die in the Twenty-First century due to religious and political deceptions. Both are connected because there are those who use the name of the Lord to advance their political agenda.

The devil managed to deceive one-third of angels to follow his own agenda of unsuccessful power grab.

"And there was war in heaven: Michael and his angels fought against the dragon; and the dragon fought and his angels And prevailed not; neither was their place found any more in heaven. And the great dragon was cast out, that old serpent, called the Devil, and Satan, which deceiveth the whole world: he was cast out into the earth, and his angels were cast out with him" (**Revelation 12:7-9 KJV**).

Interestingly, Satan is still recruiting not angels but those who are lost and confused church goers through deceptive tactics. The case in point was Demas who worked faithfully with Paul. He is referred to as a fellow laborer of Paul in **Philemon 1:24**. Then, Paul writes that the same Demas has backslidden from the church house to the outhouse figuratively.

"For Demas hath forsaken me, having loved this present world, and is departed unto Thessalonica; Crescens to Galatia, Titus unto Dalmatia" **Second Timothy 4:10 KJV**).

Demas was not the only one deceived through seduction of the "present world". Many others including Samson and Solomon who were attracted to the wrong women through deception. Solomon concluded that, all his misdeeds were all "vanity and vexation of the spirit." Alexander the coppersmith was another character who turned against Paul because he was deceived by thinking that attacking a high-profile person like Paul could result in some kind of fame.

"Alexander the coppersmith did me much evil: the Lord reward him according to his works: Of whom be thou ware also; for he hath greatly withstood our words. (**Second Timothy 4:14,15 KJV**).

Judas Iscariot's deception was surprising for he walked with Christ, saw the miracles, and was also empowered with authority to heal the sick and cast out demons. Yet was deceived and betrayed Christ. We are also informed that one of the end time characters will deceive many people through miracles that will be performed.

"And I beheld another beast coming up out of the earth; and he had two horns like a lamb, and he spake as a dragon. And he exerciseth all the power of the first beast before him, and causeth the earth and them which dwell therein to worship the first beast, whose deadly wound was healed. And he doeth great wonders, so that he maketh fire come down from heaven on the earth in the sight of men, And deceiveth them that dwell on the earth by the means of those miracles which he had power to do in the sight of the beast; saying to them that dwell on the earth, that they should make an image to the beast, which had the wound by a sword, and did live. And he had power to give life unto the image of the beast, that the image of the beast should both speak, and cause that as many as would not worship the image of the beast should be killed.

And he causeth all, both small and great, rich, and poor, free and bond, to receive a mark in their right hand, or in their foreheads: And that no man might buy or sell, save he that had the mark, or the name of the beast, or the number of his name. Here is wisdom. Let him that hath understanding count the number of the beast: for it is the number of a man; and his number is Six hundred threescore and six" (**Revelations 13:11-18, KJV**).

Chapter Thirteen
The Spirit of Heaviness

"Thou hast known my reproach, and my shame, and my dishonour: mine adversaries are all before thee. Reproach hath broken my heart; and I am full of heaviness: and I looked for some to take pity, but there was none; and for comforters, but I found none" (**Psalms 69:19,20 KJV**).

Heaviness of the spirit is usually the combination of different things that cause pain, shame, sorrow, and puts one in a gloomy mood. It is a form of mental or emotional illness. The Psalmist is asking for help but there was no one around to give him any kind of support. The New Lexicon Webster's dictionary defines depression as the "**condition of being less active than usual or a state of low mental vitality.**" The Word of God tells us about depression and the solution to it. Depression is not an easy word to define; for what may be depressing to one, may not be depressing for another person. One of the bible characters who suffered from depression was David. "Reproach hath broken my heart, and I am full of heaviness; and I looked for some to take pity, but there was one; and for comforters, but I found none" (**Ps. 69:20**). David was depressed on a number of occasions; one of which was the news of the death of his son Absalom.

"The king was shaken by the news. He went to the room above the gate and cried. "My son Absalom!" he said as he went. "My son, my son Absalom! I wish I had died in your place! Absalom, my son, my son!" (**Second Samuel 18:33**) God's Word Translation. The loss of a loved one, among other things such as divorce and financial losses can result in depression. David was also depressed and he needed a positive change emotionally after Uriah's murder which he facilitated.

"Purge me with hyssop, and I shall be clean: wash me, and I shall be whiter than snow. Make me to hear joy and gladness; that the bones which thou hast broken may rejoice. Hide thy face from my sins and blot out all mine iniquities. Create in me a clean heart, O God; and renew a right spirit within me" (**Psalms 51:7-10 KJV**).

David's depression was caused by guilt, sin, shame, and condemnation. He was confronted by the prophet concerning his bad behavior.

"And Nathan said to David, Thou art the man. Thus, saith the LORD God of Israel, I anointed thee king over Israel, and I delivered thee out of the hand of Saul; And I gave thee thy master's house, and thy master's wives into thy bosom, and gave thee the house of Israel and of Judah; and if that had been too little, I would moreover have given unto thee such and such things. Wherefore hast thou despised the commandment of the LORD, to do evil in his sight? thou hast killed Uriah the Hittite with the sword, and hast taken his wife to be thy wife, and hast slain him with the sword of the children of Ammon" (**Second Samuel 12:7-9 KJV**).

Sometimes the depressed person may be strong enough to take some positive steps such as with David when he had to encourage himself. We are told that David was distressed because the Amalekites destroyed his properties and took the women captives including his two wives. On top of all that, his followers blamed him for the calamity, and "spoke of stoning him". The author of the book of Samuel tells us that "David and the people with him lifted up their voice and wept, until they had no more power to weep" (**First Samuel 30:4**) KJV. It is not unusual for a depressed person to cry, but it is something different when a man cries and in this case many men cried together "until they were too weak to cry anymore" (**First Samuel 30:4**).

There are different reactions to depression. Some cry when depressed, do house chores too many times, and some turn to alcohol or other sexual actions that provide temporary relief but long-time regret. In addition, some eat a lot, while some lose their appetite for food. Then, there are those that shop for things they don't really need, and a few shoplift until caught. Statistics show that women suffering from postnatal depression usually become insecure, and sometimes feel unloved by their spouses. The medical profession has also associated physical infirmities as one of the causes of depression, and vice versa. Dr. Kurt Koch points out that "**A low calcium concentration in the blood can produce visionary experience, and a low hormone concentration can produce a**

severe depressive state." For example, Jaundice which causes the white side to turn yellow has also been associated with depression. One of the most ignored cause of depression is demonic attacks to create instability in one's life. There are situations when several members of one family suffer from mood issues due to influence from unclean spirits that have attached to the family. Some of the people that are being treated for psychosis are suffering from demonic attacks. The work of God points out that the devil is an oppressor and wants to steal the joy and the progress so as to make life miserable for as many people as possible. "God anointed Jesus who went about doing good and healing all that are oppressed o the devil; (**Acts 10: 38**) KJV. Many people are taking antidepressants to help them cope with "irritability, Feelings of guilt. Worthlessness or helplessness, Loss of interest or pleasure in hobbies and activities, Changes in energy levels, appetite, sleep patterns, concentration, and self-worth"

There are professionals such as psychologists and psychiatrists that can help tremendously but are also limited and sometimes the doctor honestly tells a patient that he cannot find anything wrong with the patient.

We sometimes blame the weather for certain moods and sometimes we classify some people as always moody, or we say that he or she is " **depressing to be around** ". Have you sometimes suddenly shifted into a sad mood without knowing the reason why? Many people have but have overlooked the obvious reasons. Some of these mysterious mood changes are demonic, not all but can be controlled once the truth is known. Demonic attacks that lead to depression are usually due to a portal that someone in the family steps into. Demons use our thought-life as avenues of influence as they have great powers of suggestions. Thoughts are planted unaware of the source and then corresponding actions happen. An un-renewed mind is especially more prone to their influence than a renewed mind or one who is spiritually minded. Our thought life can be protected by the "**helmet of salvation**" (Eph. 6:17); and be accountable to a self-appointed sponsor. The sponsor should be allowed to point out when a behavior is questionable so that a conscious adjustment can be made. The process may be frustrating to the one being monitored but is profitable if patience is allowed to work.

"And they may come to their senses and escape from the snare of the devil, after being captured by him to do his will" (**Second Timothy 2:26**) English Standard Version.

Depression is a trap or snare that can be entered into unaware. It is associated with synonyms such as "blue devils, blues, dejection, desolation, despond, despondence, despondency, disconsolateness", However, the condition is not hopeless. There is no one solution that fits all because each person is uniquely different, and actions and reactions are also different.

Despondency has different level of activities, but the common symptoms include: "Sadness, tiredness, trouble focusing or concentrating, unhappiness, anger, irritability, frustration, loss of interest in pleasurable or fun activities, sleep issues (too much or too little), no energy, craving unhealthy foods, anxiety, and isolation."

In addition, skipping church services, and holding back financial support to their churches should be added to the common symptoms of depression. Unfortunately, depression also kills because a noticeable number of people have contemplated suicide, and some unfortunately did succeed in taking their lives. For example, in 2020, data shows that, "12.2 million adults seriously thought about suicide, 3.2 million adults made a plan, 1.2 million adults attempted it" and 45,979 people died by suicide. That is one death every Eleven minutes.

The Psalmist cries out that, "The sorrows of death compassed me, and the pains of hell gat hold upon me: I found trouble and sorrow" (**Psalms 116:3 KJV**).

The Psalmist felt trapped with terrible emotions, but he didn't feel hopeless because the next couple of verses reveal that help was available and is still available to those who feel trapped:

"Then called I upon the name of the LORD; O LORD, I beseech thee, deliver my soul. Gracious is the LORD, and righteous; yea, our God is merciful. The LORD preserveth the simple: I was brought low, and he helped me" (**Psalms 116:4-6 KJV**).

There is direct and indirect help from God through the professional care givers, church support, friends, and some family members who find themselves to be the caregivers. But patience is necessary on every side due to the seeming challenges in understanding the person suffering with depression. The family caregiver living with a person suffering with depression are sometimes faced with the conundrum of trying to balance their lives with their own issues and at the same time support their depressed loved ones, without feeling trapped in the vicious circle. Is there any resource for family caregivers? The answer is an affirmative yes. The gospel according to Mark tells us of a father whose son was faced with many challenges and sought the help of Christ.

"And one of the multitudes answered and said, Master, I have brought unto thee my son, which hath a dumb spirit; And wheresoever he taketh him, he teareth him: and he foameth, and gnasheth with his teeth, and pineth away.... And ofttimes it hath cast him into the fire, and into the waters, to destroy him: but if thou canst do anything, have compassion on us, and help us." (**Mark 9:17,18,22 KJV**).

Children can also suffer from depression for the data show the signs of depression in children and teens include "**changes in appetite or weight, feeling or appearing depressed, sad, tearful, or irritable, fatigue or perceived lack of energy, feeling guilty or ashamed and having more trouble concentrating.**" (American Academy of Child and Adolescent Psychiatry)

It is therefore, very clear that family caregivers need support as well, "have compassion on us and help us" was the father's cry. Caregivers has to be careful about where to get help for themselves. When David was in distress, he said that "he looked for pity...but there was none" (**Psalm 69: 20**). David's first mistake is common among many people today; he first wallowed in self-pity and then looked for "**comforters**" in the wrong place. Then, when he found out that man could not help him he said, "I will lift up mine eyes unto the hills. From whence cometh my help? My help cometh form the Lord" (**Psalm 121:1,2**). David made another important move. He "encouraged himself in the Lord his God" (**1 Sam. 30:6**). Sometimes, we have to encourage ourselves in the Lord. Those who do not know God turn to alcohol, and or drugs for uplifting, and their situations usually become worse. We can become encouraged by simply remembering that it was God that brought us this far, especially when we remember certain situations that we had considered to be hopeless. But God gave us hope in seemingly hopeless situations. David encouraged himself by recognizing that God is a "very present help in trouble . Therefore, will not we fear" (**Psalm 46:1,2**). Fear is a negative force which clouds the mind, and one needs to refuse to be fearful, and instead have faith in God. Secondly, David says "in my distress I called on the Lord" (Psalm 18:6); and after he called on the Lord, he waited on the Lord. Most emotional healings are progressive, and it is required that we patiently wait on the Lord. "Wait on the Lord...and he shall strengthen thine heart. Wait I say on the Lord" (**Psalm 27:4**). The writer of Hebrews says, "Cast not away, therefore your confidence, For ye have need of patience that, after ye have done the will of God, ye might receive the promise' (Hebrews 10:35, 36). Job in his most difficult times of his life waited on God; "in all the days of my appointed time will I wait, till my change come" (**Job 14:14**).

Changes come when we make the choice to reject some of the depressing thoughts for the bible suggests the right-kind of thinking such as:

"Finally, brethren, whatsoever things are true, whatsoever things are honest, whatsoever things are just, whatsoever things are pure, whatsoever things are lovely, whatsoever things are of good report; if there be any virtue, and if there be any praise, think on these things" (**Philippians 4:8**) KJV.

Also, Apostle Paul's instruction to the Corinthians Christians is to reject and overthrow: "reasonings and every high thing that lifts itself up against the knowledge of God, and leading captive every thought into the obedience of the Christ" (**Second Corinthians 10:5**) KJV

The efforts to bring thoughts into captivity is a continual process, not a one-time deal. First, one must decide if a thought lines up with the Word of God. Is the thought leading away from God or towards God? Is it a anger provoking thought? Fear provoking? Or is it faith and praise provoking?

""I was told something secretly and heard something whispered in my ear. With disturbing thoughts from visions in the night, when deep sleep falls on people, fear and trembling came over me, and all my bones shook" (**Job 4:12-14**) God's Word Version.

A "**disturbing thought**" can come from what is read or heard from the pulpit and it is good if it leads to repentance towards God.

"If my letter made you uncomfortable, I'm not sorry. But since my letter did make you uncomfortable for a while, I was sorry. But I'm happy now, not because I made you uncomfortable, but because the distress I caused you has led you to change the way you think and act. You were distressed in a godly way, so we haven't done you any harm. In fact, to be distressed in a godly way causes people to change the way they think and act and leads them to be saved. No one can regret that. But the distress that the world causes bring only death. When you became distressed in a godly way, look at how much devotion it caused you to have. You were ready to clear yourselves of the charges against you. You were disgusted with the wrong that had been done. You were afraid. You wanted to see us. You wanted to show your concern for us. You were ready to punish the wrong that had been done. In every way you have demonstrated that you are people who are innocent in this matter" (**Second Corinthians 7:8-11**) God's Word).

In my humble opinion, the final thought on this chapter is that there is not one single thing to bring an end to depression. Having family caregivers is good, but not a cure all; church support is good but not a cure all, rejection of negative thoughts is good but not a cure all, professional help is good but not a cure all. Having God in one's life is a must and with God's help and the above listed resources life should be a whole lot smoother.

Chapter Fourteen
Why Get Healed To Loose It?

"You're well now. Stop sinning so that something worse doesn't happen to you." (**John 5:12-14**) God's Word

"The thief comes only to steal and kill and destroy. I came that they may have life and have it abundantly" (**John 10:10**) English Standard Version.

The thief mentioned in the gospel according to Apostle John chapter ten verse ten is not a common thief. He is not human but specializes in stealing intangible things and does not value life. Therefore, he kills and destroys lives. He steals things such as faith, joy, self-confidence, God-confidence, goodness, and other intangible things. Good health cannot be bought but can be stolen through ignorance and deception. Apostle John wishes Christians to be healthy. "Beloved, I wish above all things that thou mayest prosper and be in health, even as thy soul prospereth" (**3 John 1:2**) KJV. And because good health is a spiritual blessing: the thief would like to steal it form you. Provision for health and healing was made by God for His people through the sacrifice on the cross. This provision was prophesied by Prophet Isaiah centuries before Christ was born in Bethlehem.

"He is despised and rejected of men; a man of sorrows and acquainted with grief: and we hid as it were our faces from him; he was despised, and we esteemed him not. Surely, he hath borne our griefs, and carried our sorrows: yet we did esteem him stricken, smitten of God, and afflicted. But he was wounded for our transgressions, he was bruised for our iniquities: the chastisement of our peace was upon him; and with his stripes we are healed" (**Isaiah 53:3-5**) KJV.

Those in the healing ministry are faced with the conundrum of a recurrence of an illness or disease after the individual has testified to being healed or delivered. As humans, we like to find explanations for a recurrence that happens, and science has provided a few explanations, but are unable to explain all recurrent cases. For example, cancer cells that the first treatment did not remove can grow into tumors or cancer. This recurrence usually results in fear, anger, shock, and sadness. Also, science informs us that Lyme disease and spider veins can also return after treatment.

In John chapter five, we see the story of a man that had been disabled for thirty-eight years and was healed by Christ. Before the arrival of Jesus, there was no one to help him, for everyone at his location needed help themselves. His situation appeared hopeless for thirty-eight years. It is important to note that the help that this man needed was spiritual as revealed later by Christ.

His infirmity was not the result of an accident, intentional harm, or genetic disorder. He had missed thirty-eight years of mobility, fellowship with his loved ones and lost thirty-eight years of gainful employment. The people around him for thirty-eight years were also sick and physically disabled individuals. Fast forward, Jesus saw the man later in the church and recognized him and gave a warning that gives us insight why recurrence of an illness or disease can happen: "You're well now. Stop sinning so that something worse doesn't happen to you." (**John 5:14**) God's Word

This man received forgiveness for his transgression which was the source of disability. This story should not be taken as applicable to every sickness, disease, or disability. Because there are other factors that can cause the recurrence of a condition such as demonic attack.

Dr. Luke, one of the disciples of Christ and a notable physician reveals the story of a woman whose condition was the result of demonic attack. We are told that this woman had a curvature of the spine and was unable to walk straight. She was mostly looking at the ground because of her condition that was the result of demonic attack.

"Now, here is a descendant of Abraham. Satan has kept her in this condition for 18 years. Isn't it right to free her on the day of worship?" (**Luke 13:16**) God's Word Translation

Satan has the right to attack when someone steps into his territory, and many people have been attacked due to ignorance (**Hosea 4:6**). Does being set free gives immunity from future attacks? The answer is obviously no!

Please know that Satan would like to steal the joy of being healed to replace it with anger, and loss of faith in the God of the bible.

The Word of God clearly tells us that demonic spirits can attack the body with sickness, and it is important that, demons are more likely to attack a Christian than an unbeliever to discourage, and some are meant to destroy one's faith. A sickness caused by a demon requires that the demon be expelled or cast out. The demon must first be bound, then commanded authoritatively to leave. Many people have been discouraged in their affliction to find out that the sickness worsens after the prayer. Some people have wrongfully concluded that when a person remains sick after prayer, then it must not be God's will for the person to be healed. Whenever a person remains sick without any sign of relief after prayer, or whenever a person becomes worse after prayer, it is more than likely that a demonic spirit is behind the sickness. This does not negate the power of prayer because prayer works! However, a prayer of deliverance is different from a prayer for petition and other kinds of prayer. Please note that a prayer of deliverance speaks directly and authoritatively to the demons in the Name of Jesus Christ, whereas other kinds of prayer are directed to God in the Name of Jesus Christ.

Prayer is a powerful weapon against demonic forces or any adversities of life. Jesus prayed, Paul prayed, and the early church also prayed.

"And when they had prayed, the place was shaken where they were assembled together; and they were all filled with the Holy Ghost, and they spake the word of God with boldness" (Acts 4:31) KJV.

Corporate prayer in one accord gets heavens attention and God responds to the petitions.

Prayer also has a preventive component as it shields the believer from the recurrent of a sickness caused by the spirit of infirmity. Once a demonic spirit is forced out then, the person delivered has the responsibility of closing all avenues and portals of return. Among the openings are unforgiving spirit, occult involvement and other form of rebellion to God's Word.

When a demonically bound person has been set free from the spirit of infirmity, the person who was bound must not give legal grounds for the affliction to return. "I will return into my house from which I came out" is the desire of every demon that has been forced out. Demons prefer to live in a human body rather than in any other creature. This is because humans are the only created beings made in His image and likeness of God, and it gives them satisfaction to control and influence whomever they can.

"When the unclean spirit is gone out of a man, he walketh through dry places, seeking rest, and findeth none. Then he saith, I will return into my house from whence I came out; and when he is come, he findeth it empty, swept, and garnished. Then goeth he, and taketh with himself seven other spirits more wicked than himself, and they enter in and dwell there: and the last state of that man is worse than the first. Even so shall it be also unto this wicked generation" (**Matthew 12:43-45**).

The above scripture does not imply the possession of a believer upon return after expulsion. Please know that demons cannot inhabit the spirit of a believer. Because that is where the Holy Spirit exercises influence in the life of a believer, However, demons can "**legally**" operate in the body of a believer when there is an opportunity to do so. "**Legally**" means when a person wanders into the jurisdiction of demons knowingly or ignorantly is an opportunity for demons to attack. Demonic jurisdictions range from unforgiveness, to dabbling in the occult. Also, an unrenewed mind is an avenue of influence by demons. That is why Paul's letter to the church at Rome is relevant.

"Be ye transformed by the renewing of your mind, that ye may prove what is that good, and acceptable, and perfect, will of God" (Romans 12:2) KJV.

Renewing the mind is a process that may take some time. Those who have computers understand reprograming a computer or updating a computer to function properly. Many Christians understand that when a person accepts Jesus as Lord and Savior, the human spirit becomes regenerated immediately, but the mind and body remains the same. The mind can be progressively renewed to conform with the Word of God. However, the body which Paul describes as "**corruptible**" and "**vile**" remains the same until we exchange it with a spiritual body at the coming of the Lord (**1 Corinthians 15:53,54**). Until then, demons can hide and influence a believer through the corruptible body if allowed. Another legal ground for demons to return after being forced out is through open rebellion to spiritual authority such as a pastor. Unfortunately, when demons return, they bring extra demons for insulation so that it will be more difficult to force them out next time around. A person who has been delivered must occupy his thoughts with the Word of God and things that are pure, just and of good report as instructed in the epistle to the Philippians chapter four verse eight. In addition, Paul recommends wearing the **"Helmet of Salvation"** to protect the believer from the consequence of ungodly thoughts. The helmet of salvation is designed to protect the believer's thought life from demonic power of suggestions. However, the helmet must be worn to be effective.

Another preventive maintenance is to avoid negative words from our mouth.

"Thou art snared with the words of thy mouth, thou art taken with the words of thy mouth" (**Proverbs 6:2 KJV**).

The word "**snared**" means trapped. Whenever a negative word is spoken consistently from our mouth, we automatically give the **"prince of the power of the air"** permission to make it a reality. An adult who has been told several times since childhood that she was stupid reacted negatively to the word "**stupid**" and believed that she was stupid. The influence of words on a person cannot be overemphasized.

The Word of God says, "death and life are in the power of the tongue" (**Proverbs 18:21**). This means that a life can be shaped with words that results in the action of a person with time. Words are like a boomerang which can return to the thrower. Therefore, instead of negative words, biological or spiritual parent ought to pronounce life on their children repeatedly. Words are confident builders on individual or a team.

The reference to Satan being is a "**thief**" in John 10:10 is significant. A thief by nature looks for an opportunity to pick up valuable things that belong to someone else. Therefore, it is wise to protect one's valuables including non-tangible valuables such as healing, health and peace of mind.

Chapter Fifteen
Who Is your daddy?

"Ye are of your father the devil, and the lusts of your father ye will do. He was a murderer from the beginning, and abode not in the truth, because there is no truth in him. When he speaketh a lie, he speaketh of his own: for he is a liar, and the father of it" (**John 8:44**) KJV.

Deoxyribonucleic acid (DNA), also called **"the molecule of life"** has been used to solve crimes by identifying the culprit. Also important is the use of DNA testing to identify the biological father of a child when in doubt.

Paternity testing has become very popular in this generation because of peace of mind for many parents as well as the children. There are four **"fathers"** identified in the bible. First is the biological, and the second and third are spiritual fathers. The fourth refers to descendants of an individual such as written in John chapter eight.

"They answered and said unto him, Abraham is our father. Jesus saith unto them, If ye were Abraham's children, ye would do the works of Abraham" (**John 8:39 KJV**).

The DNA, when used figuratively can be used to identify the children of each of the fathers. For example, **"the works of Abraham"** as Jesus cast a doubt on the Jews that claim to be Abraham's children.

Similarly, Jesus clearly tells us that Satan is also a **"father"** and his figurative children will follow his footsteps identified by what they do. "A good tree cannot bring forth evil fruit, neither can a corrupt tree bring forth good fruit is hewn down, and cast into the fire, wherefore by their fruits ye shall know them" (**Matthew 7:18-20**) KJV.

The **"Fruit"** refers to the products of a tree and symbolically point to the DNA of either Satan or The Heavenly Father.

Who is your daddy? can also be seen in Paul's writing regarding the DNA of individuals prior to the return of Christ.

Paul prophesied concerning the personality traits that will be seen in people' even among those who profess the Name of the Lord: but woe unto these by whom they are fulfilled.

"For men shall be lovers of their own selves, covetous, boasters, proud, blasphemers, disobedient to parents, unthankful, unholy, without natural affection, trucebreakers, false accusers, incontinent, fierce, despisers of those that are good, Traitors, heady, high-minded, lovers of pleasures more than lovers of God; Having a form of godliness but denying the power thereof: from such turn away. For of this sort are they which creep into houses, and lead captive silly women laden with sins, led away with divers lusts, Ever learning, and never able to come to the knowledge of the truth" (**Second Timothy 3:2-7**) KJV.

LOVERS OF THEIR OWN SELVES; The interpreter's Bible says. **"Self-love is the fundamental sin and the source of all other because it substitutes sinful man for God. The truly religious man puts God at the center of his life. "** "**Lovers of self**" are those who are egocentric and fail to prioritize the things of God above their own needs.

COVETOUS: This is the doctrine of Ahab, who became unhappy until he possessed another man's belongings. Any time a person develops a strong desire for another's property, it is an indication of a covetous spirit. A spoiled child can easily develop this personality if allowed to continue without being checked. A grown man with a covetous spirit is as dangerous as an armed robber.

BOASTERS: The interpreter's Bible tells us that the Greek word translated into boasters includes the "idea of making false pretense." People under this category like to brag about what they do for others, and how much they spend, to gain recognition. Boasters are exhibitionists, who will stop being generous if they are not allowed to be ostentatious. A pastor once said of a woman that was in his congregation who bragged about everything she did for the church and expected to have a position of influence in the church. She left after she found out that her Pastor could not be bought.

PROUD; One of the things that God hates is 'a proud look' (**Proverbs 6:17**), and we are also told that "God resisteth the proud" (**James 4:6; First Peter 5:5**). This means that God does not look kindly to those who exemplify pride. Some may remember that Lucifer fell from heaven partly because of pride.

How art thou fallen from heaven, O Lucifer, son of the morning! how art thou cut down to the ground, which didst weaken the nations! For thou hast said in thine heart, I will ascend into heaven, I will exalt my throne above the stars of God: I will sit also upon the mount of the congregation, in the sides of the north: I will ascend above the heights of the clouds; I will be like the most High.

Yet thou shalt be brought down to hell, to the sides of the pit. They that see thee shall narrowly look upon thee, and consider thee, saying, Is this the man that made the earth to tremble, that did shake kingdoms (**Isaiah 14:12-16**) KJV

BLASPHEMERS: These are people who speak evil of God or man. Of course, blasphemy against the Holy Spirit is an unpardonable sin.

"Wherefore I say unto you, All manner of sin and blasphemy shall be forgiven unto men: but the blasphemy against the Holy Ghost shall not be forgiven unto men. And whosoever speaketh a word against the Son of man, it shall be forgiven him: but whosoever speaketh against the Holy Ghost, it shall not be forgiven him, neither in this world, neither in the world to come" (**Matthew 12:31.32**) KJV

DISOBEDIENT TO PARENTS; There are biological parents as well as spiritual parents. That is, those who serve as senior pastors are the spiritual parents. The writer of Hebrews gives instruction concerning spiritual authority by saying:

"Obey them that have the rule over you and submit yourselves: for they watch for your souls, as they that must give account, that they may do it with joy, and not with grief: for that is unprofitable for you" (**Hebrews 13:17**) KJV.

If there is any time in the history of mankind when children are rebellious to parental authority, it is now. This is because there are so many more distractions facing the children of this generation than any other time.

UNTHANKFUL: Remember the story of the ten lepers? After being healed, nine did not return to express their gratitude to Jesus. The spirit of those nine lepers is more influential in our times than at any other time. Have you ever come across people who act as if God and everybody owes them something?

UNHOLY; Holiness is a lifestyle that involves navigating through the "**straight and narrow path**". It involves walking in love to others and being an example of what Christ did in His earthly ministry.

"But as he which hath called you is holy, so be ye holy in all manner of conversation; Because it is written, Be ye holy; for I am holy" (**First Peter 1:15,16**) KJV.

WITHOUT NATURAL AFFECTION, The natural affection of parents for their children seems to be in question as children are being abandoned and left to fend for themselves. The unselfish love that David and Jonathan had for each other may be lacking in this generation. Bestiality is an unnatural affection and the interpreter's Bible describes the people without natural affection as "unfeeling, callous with hard and dry hearts".

TRUCE BREAKERS: These are people who are implacable and who refuse to enjoy the fellowship of others because of their own hangups. A young preacher told me of several efforts he made to placate one of the families in his church without success. This is typical of the spirit of Truce breakers. They are the thorns in a pastor's flesh.

FALSE ACCUSERS: These are slanderers that are responsible for planting rumors and sowing discord and sometimes causing church splits.

INCONTINENT: Sexual perversion, with no regard to sexual morality. In our times, **"hard-core pornography"** and child pornography are on the increase. The National Coalition Against Pornography says, **"Hard-core pornography is an extreme form of pornography that depicts the most explicit and offensive representations of sexual activity imaginable, including the glamorization of the kidnapping and rape of women and sexual molestation of children".**

FIERCE: wild or savage, brutal, cruel.

DESPISERS OF THOSE THAT ARE GOOD: The goal is to discourage the walk and progress of other Christians who are interested in progress and helping others.

TRAITORS: People who betray the confidence of others in them. Treacherous, not to be trusted.

HEADY: reckless, rash, stopping at nothing to gain their ends.

HIGH-MINDED: swollen with self-conceit, **"wrapped up in conceit and folly"** or self-proclaimed importance.

LOVERS OF PLEASURE MORE THAN LOVERS OF GOD: They will be lovers of pleasures and vain amusements more than and rather than lovers of God.

HAVING A FORM OF GODLINESS BUT DENYING...: These are people with religious spirits. People under the influence of religious spirits are often difficult to minister because they are very dogmatic, and incorrigible. This is the reason for Paul's advice to Timothy, to keep his distance from such individuals. "They profess to know God: but in works they deny him. Being abominable, and disobedient, and unto every good work reprobate" (**Titus 1:16**).

It has been said that "**the apple doesn't fall too far from the tree.**" The biological son of King David is Solomon who has the DNA of his father. King David offended God by his action with Bathsheba. Solomon also offended God by his taste in the women he chose. Solomon married three hundred women and seven hundred concubines. Many of them came from pagan countries. It took Solomon a long time to find out that everything he acquired including his taste of a thousand women did not fill his void.

"I explored ways to make myself feel better by drinking wine. I also explored ways to do some foolish things. During all that time, wisdom continued to control my mind. I was able to determine whether this was good for mortals to do during their brief lives under heaven. I accomplished some great things: I built houses for myself. I planted vineyards for myself. I made gardens and parks for myself. I planted every kind of fruit tree in them. I made pools to water the forest of growing trees. I bought male and female slaves. In addition, slaves were born in my household. I owned more herds and flocks than anyone in Jerusalem before me. I also gathered silver and gold for myself. I gathered the treasures of kings and provinces. I provided myself with male and female singers and the pleasures men have with one concubine after another. So, I grew richer than anyone in Jerusalem before me. Yet, my wisdom remained with me. If something appealed to me, I did it. I allowed myself to have any pleasure I wanted, since I found pleasure in my work. This was my reward for all my hard work. But when I turned to look at all that I had accomplished and all the hard work I had put into it, I saw that it was all pointless. It was like trying to catch the wind. I gained nothing from any of my accomplishments under the sun" (**Ecclesiastes 2:3-11**) God's Word.

The DNA of King David can be linked to Solomon because Solomon, like his father, wanted something new, or better someone different. David had an insatiable thirst which transferred to Solomon. It was at sunset, perhaps he was restless and while walking on the topmost part of the palace saw a "**forbidden fruit**" figuratively because the woman belongs to another man named Uriah.

Bathsheba was a beautiful woman who was perhaps a lonely housewife because her husband was fighting a war for the king and country. David was the king who yielded to his flesh when he saw Bathsheba taking a bath in a topless bathroom. When is it enough for the flesh? The answer is obvious. The flesh can never be satisfied. After Bathsheba came other wives and concubines. David had at least eight wives and we are informed that he took on more concubines and wives from Jerusalem.

"David married more concubines and wives from Jerusalem after he had come there from Hebron, and he fathered more sons and daughters" (**Second Samuel 5:13**) God's Word translation.

It is therefore not surprising that Solomon followed in his father's footsteps. Fast forward, Jesus disputed the claim of the Jews who claim that they are descendants of Abraham.

"Jesus saith unto them, If ye were Abraham's children, ye would do the works of Abraham" (**John 8:39**) KJV.

Abraham walked by faith and was obedient to God's commands and instructions. The Jews of Christ's time focused on how they will destroy Christ. Therefore, Jesus pointed out that they behaved not like Abraham, therefore reflected the personalities of Satan.

"Ye are of your father the devil, and the lusts of your father ye will do. He was a murderer from the beginning, and abode not in the truth, because there is no truth in him. When he speaketh a lie, he speaketh of his own: for he is a liar, and the father of it." (**John 8:44**) KJV.

Chapter Sixteen
The Overcoming Pastor

A Pastor friend lived in a parsonage with his family that was built on the church property right in front of the church burial ground. During our fellowship, I noticed the burial ground and asked him if he was ever bothered by the burial ground behind the parsonage. His response, **"the dead does not bother me only the living."** It was an interesting response and almost every Pastor can identify with what my late friend said. There are different personalities in every congregation and if we are to look at Christ twelve-member congregation as the model should give an insight to Pastoral ministry. When Christ was in the Garden of Gethsemane in praying, the few that He took with Him were asleep and not watching with Him.

"And he took with him Peter and the two sons of Zebedee and began to be sorrowful and very heavy. Then saith he unto them, My soul is exceeding sorrowful, even unto death: tarry ye here, and watch with me. And he went a little further, and fell on his face, and prayed, saying, O my Father, if it be possible, let this cup pass from me: nevertheless, not as I will, but as thou wilt. And he cometh unto the disciples, and findeth them asleep, and saith unto Peter, What, could ye not watch with me one hour? Watch and pray, that ye enter not into temptation: the spirit indeed is willing, but the flesh is weak. He went away again the second time, and prayed, saying, O my Father, if this cup may not pass away from me, except I drink it, thy will be done. And he came and found them asleep again: for their eyes were heavy. And he left them, and went away again, and prayed the third time, saying the same words.

Then cometh he to his disciples, and saith unto them, Sleep on now, and take your rest: behold, the hour is at hand, and the Son of man is betrayed into the hands of sinners" (**Matthew 26:37-45**) KJV.

What about Judas who betrayed Him? Peter who denied knowing Him and Thomas who was skeptical of His resurrection?

"Now Peter sat without in the palace: and a damsel came unto him, saying, Thou also wast with Jesus of Galilee. But he denied before them all, saying, I know not what thou sayest. And when he was gone out into the porch, another maid saw him, and said unto them that were there, This fellow was also with Jesus of Nazareth. And again, he denied with an oath, I do not know the man. And after a while came unto him, they that stood by, and said to Peter, Surely, thou also art one of them; for thy speech bewrayeth thee. Then began he to curse and to swear, saying, I know not the man. And immediately the cock crew. And Peter remembered the word of Jesus, which said unto him, Before the cock crow, thou shalt deny me thrice. And he went out and wept bitterly" (**Matthew 26:69-75**) KJV.

John also tells us about a day when Jesus was misunderstood by many of His disciples.

"From that time many of his disciples went back and walked no more with him. Then said Jesus unto the twelve, Will ye also go away?" (**John 6:66,67**)

Pastors can easily be understood and therefore, each Pastor must develop a "**thick skin**" because the job requires understanding that people can be unpredictable from time to time. Case in point was Demas (**Second Timothy 4:10**).

Apostle Paul in his letters to Timothy and Titus describes what can be described as the qualifications for leadership withing the Body of Christ:

"This is a true saying, If a man desire the office of a bishop, he desireth a good work. A bishop then must be blameless, the husband of one wife, vigilant, sober, of good behaviour, given to hospitality, apt to teach.

Not given to wine, no striker, not greedy of filthy lucre; but patient, not a brawler, not covetous; One that ruleth well his own house, having his children in subjection with all gravity; (For if a man know not how to rule his own house, how shall he take care of the church of God?)

Not a novice, lest being lifted up with pride he fall into the condemnation of the devil. Moreover, he must have a good report of them which are without; lest he fall into reproach and the snare of the devil" (**First Timothy 3:2-7**) KJV.

- the husband of one wife
- above reproach
- temperate and self-controlled

- respectable
- hospitable
- able to teach
- not given to much wine
- not violent but gentle
- not quarrelsome
- not a lover of money able to manage his own money well and see that his children obey him with proper respect
- must not be a recent convert
- must have a good reputation with outsiders, so that he will not fall into disgrace and into the devil's trap
- not overbearing
- not pursuing dishonest gain
- holy and disciplined
- must hold firmly to the trustworthy message as it has been taught, so that he can encourage others by sound doctrine and refute those who oppose it, (**1 Tim3:2-7; Titus 1;6-9**)
- Above all these, a pastor must love people, and understand and practice what Jesus says, "**Feed my lambs**" and" Feed my sheep" (**John 21:15-17**). It is important that pastors observe these passages of scriptures for their own education, I was not in the habit if looking at these qualifications, but I have found them to be useful. "Thou, therefore, who teaches another, teaches thou not thyself? Thou that preaches a man should not steal, dost thou steal? Thou that sayest a man should not commit adultery, dost thou commit adultery? (**Romans 2:21,22**)

In the letters to the pastors in Asia, John uses the expression, "he that overcometh" in each of the seven letters and as well as in Chapter Twenty-one verse seven can be found in the book of **Revelation 2:7, 11, 17, 26; 3:5, 12, 21**). To overcome is to prevail, to get the victory, and to conquer, Every Christian including the spiritual authorities has to overcome to receive the rewards. Everyone needs to understand the biblical approach to being referred to as an overcomer. First, the Bible says that a Believer has already overcome because of faith in Christ's death, burial, and resurrection.

"For whatsoever is born of God overcometh the world: and this is the victory that overcometh the world, even our faith. 1 Jn 5:5 Who is he that overcometh the world, but he that believeth that Jesus is the Son of God?" (**First John 5:4,5**) KJV

However, one must go through experience. For example, one has been given a restaurant gift certificate, but has not yet utilized the gift certificate. Dining in such a restaurant is to experience the gift of the food. Similarly, there is the second part being an overcomer through experience.

Each person has to face trials, tests and temptations that are uniquely designed. Pastors, like ever one else, must overcome temptations, the lust of the flesh, the lust to the eyes, and the pride of life. Everyone has to learn how to react to other people's actions, which may not be pleasant. Resisting the devil is everybody's responsibility including the spiritual leaders. Paul writes from experience, "let him that thinks he stands take heed lest he fall" (**First Corinthian 10:12**).

The devil's attack is sometimes directed towards the preacher's integrity and character. The preacher's integrity is connected to the integrity of God's word as viewed by many. "How shall they believe whom they have not heard? And how shall they hear without the preacher" (**Romans 10:14**) KJV.

The burden to uphold the banner and avoid being misunderstood lies with those who have been given the charge of the gospel of Christ. Being misunderstood is part of the job but one still has to walk the line. Jesus of course was misunderstood and many of his disciples left him as reported in John chapter six verse sixty-six.

"Therefore, see then, that ye walk circumspectly, not as fools but as wise, redeeming because time, because the days are evil. Wherefore, be ye not unwise but understanding what the will of the Lord is." (**Ephesians 5:15-17**).

The will of God is that the Church survives demonic attacks, especially those individuals in leadership positions. "Upon this rock I will build my church, and the gates of hell shall not prevail against it." (**Matthew 16:18 KJV**).

The church is many members with personalities and denominations and each constituent will need to understand the need to overlook the things that separate us such the doctrine of Trinity versus "Oneness" and which day has been sanctioned for worship. The church has to focus on what and who should be the focus.

"Endeavoring to keep the unity of the Spirit in the bond of peace. There is one body, and one Spirit, even as ye are called in one hope of your calling; One Lord, one faith, one baptism, One God and Father of all, who is above all, and through all, and in you all. But unto every one of us is given grace according to the measure of the gift of Christ" (**Ephesians 4:3-7**) KJV.

It has been said that "Old habits die hard" This is true for individuals, organizations, cultures and the list goes on. We cannot treat our grown adult children as babies because they are grown. Also, as one grows physically, the diet and the taste bud changes as well.

Apostle Paul in his letter to those in Corinth writes:

"When I was a child, I spake as a child, I understood as a child, I thought as a child: but when I became a man, I put away childish things. For now, we see through a glass, darkly; but then face to face: now I know in part; but then shall I know even as also I am known. And now abideth faith, hope, charity, these three; but the greatest of these is charity" (**First Corinthians 13:11-13**) KJV.

How does one overcome or specifically how does a Pastor live an overcoming experience? Learn the following "Eleven Commandments."

- First, take life one day at a time trusting on the guidance of the Holy Spirit.
- Second, do not be afraid to push the reset button and start over.
- Third, be open-minded.
- Fourth, do not be afraid to choose new friends who may see things differently.
- Fifth, continue to study the Word of God and allow the Holy Spirit to illuminate the mind.
- Sixth, understand that seasons bring about changes.
- Seventh, enjoy life, enjoy your family and friends!
- Eighth, learn how to handle money. It is an asset but can also be a trap.

- Ninth, learn to be a multi-tasker. Don't neglect family when trying to be a successful pastor.
- Tenth, treat everybody as you would like to be treated.
- Eleventh, accidents happen in life, and people will come and go either by death or misunderstanding. Let God be the constant factor in life.

Chapter Seventeen
The Devil's Strategies and Weapons

"And our adversaries said, They shall not know, neither see, till we come in the midst among them, and slay them, and cause the work to cease" (**Nehemiah 4:11**) KJV.

The original plan and ultimate desire of Satan is to be like God. He failed at his first attempt when Michael and angels in good standing fought against Satan and the fallen angels as recorded in chapter twelve of the book of revelation.

"How art thou fallen from heaven, O Lucifer, son of the morning! how art thou cut down to the ground, which didst weaken the nations! For thou hast said in thine heart, I will ascend into heaven, I will exalt my throne above the stars of God: I will sit also upon the mount of the congregation, in the sides of the north: I will ascend above the heights of the clouds; I will be like the most High.

He tried to carry out his insurrection against the rule of God through mutiny which failed. Satan can never be like the God, because of several factors. First, he is a liar, and is not capable of telling the truth. Therefore, he operates through lies and deceit. Such was the case with the deception of Eve in the garden of Eden.

Second, God is the life-giver, but the devil is a murderer who wants to take the lives of God's children either through ignorance or instigation of conflicts. The Devil instigated the first bloodshed in the bible. The killing of Abel by his own brother has Satan's fingerprint all over it.

Third, God is omniscient, and nothing surprises Him. The Devil, on the other hand, can never be omniscient so his strategy is limited to historical facts and guesses.

Fourth, the devil's strategy is to frustrate and discourage the Workers of Righteousness.

"But it came to pass, that when Sanballat, and Tobiah, and the Arabians, and the Ammonites, and the Ashdodites, heard that the walls of Jerusalem were made up, and that the breaches began to be stopped, then they were very wroth, And conspired all of them together to come and to fight against Jerusalem, and to hinder it". (**Nehemiah 4:7,8**) KJV

Satan's strategy includes hinderance of progress through accusations. Apostle John refers to Satan as the "accuser of our brethren" (**Revelation 12:10**). False accusations can destroy reputations, families and break up of churches.

"Divide and Conquer" (D&C) strategy is also employed by Satan to create havoc of all kinds. This D&C strategy includes the sowing of strife, divisions, and envy among the people.

"My friends, you are acting like the people of this world. That's why I could not speak to you as a spiritual people. You are like babies as far as your faith in Christ is concerned. So, I had to treat you like babies and feed you milk. You could not take solid food, and you still cannot,

because you are not yet spiritual. You are jealous and argue with each other. This proves that you are not spiritual and that you are acting like the people of this world. Some of you say that you follow me, and others claim to follow Apollos. Aren't that how ordinary people behaving? Apollos and I are merely servants who helped you to have faith. It was the Lord who made it all happen. I planted the seeds, Apollos watered them, but God made them sprout and grow. What matters isn't those who planted or watered, but God who made the plants grow" (**First Corinthian 3:1-7**) Contemporary English Version.

What really matters now is the political and religious divisions that have risen to an unprecedented level. There is now the demonization of others that do not believe the same way. Also, the demonization of others that may be of another race. There is name calling and worse, there is an associated violence. It has been reported of attacks on others because of their religious and political beliefs. Also, attacks in places of worship and on individuals that look different. The divider in chief is the devil, the "**god of this world**" whose reign will soon come to an end.

Chapter Eighteen
Relevance of Ancient Tribes

"And the LORD was With Judah: and he drove out the inhabitants of the mountains: but could not drive out the inhabitants of the valley, because they had chariots of iron" (**Judges 1:19**)

Judah was the son. of Israel by Leah, the unloved wife of Jacob. Judah is credited with saving the life of Joseph the dreamer. The name Judah became synonymous with the Southern Kingdom of Israel when the nation was divided into two. Also, Jesus descended from the tribe of Judah.

This same tribe of Judah was not successful in driving out the inhabitants of the valley. Those in the valley should have been easy targets due to their location. So, what was the problem with Judah? Could it be partly due to fear, and unbelief. Could it be because the tribe of Judah did not want to enter combat without the tribe of Simeon, even though God promised to be with Judah? Is it any different today with Christians that act out of fear because of circumstances? There should be no doubt that God will always keep His promises, and faith is necessary to hold on to His Word regardless of the circumstance. "And he brought us out from hence, that he might bring us in, to give us the land which he sware unto our fathers" (**Deuteronomy 6:23**) KJV. The promised land, however, was not uninhabited. There were other people who happened to be the enemies of Israel. These includes "the Hittites, the Girgashites, the Amorites, the Canaanites, and the Perizzites, and the Hivites, and the Jebusites, seven nations greater and mightier than thou" (**Deuteronomy 7:1**) KJV. Some of these enemies of Israel lived on the plains, some on the mountains, and some in the valley.

The Hivites

Associated with deception. The Hivites representatives disguised themselves to get a peace treaty from Joshua for self-preservation.

"And when the inhabitants of Gibeon heard what Joshua had done unto Jericho and to Ai, They did work wilily, and went and made as if they had been ambassadors, and took old sacks upon their asses, and wine bottles, old, and rent, and bound up; And old shoes and clouted upon their feet, and old garments upon them; and all the bread of their provision was dry and mouldy. And they went to Joshua unto the camp at Gilgal, and said unto him, and to the men of Israel, We be come from a far country: now therefore make ye a league with us. And the men of Israel said unto the Hivites, Peradventure ye dwell among us; and how shall we make a league with you? And they said unto Joshua, "We are thy servants. And Joshua said unto them, Who are ye? and from whence come ye? And they said unto him, From a very far country thy servants are come because of the name of the LORD thy God: for we have heard the fame of him, and all that he did in Egypt, And all that he did to the two kings of the Amorites, that were beyond Jordan, to Sihon king of Heshbon, and to Og king of Bashan, which was at Ashtaroth. Wherefore our elders and all the inhabitants of our country spake to us, saying, Take victuals with you for the journey, and go to meet them, and say unto them, We are your servants: therefore, now make ye a league with us. This our bread we took hot for our provision out of our houses on the day we came forth to go unto you; but now, behold, it is dry, and it is mouldy: And these bottles of wine, which we filled, were new; and behold, they be rent: and these our garments and our shoes are become old by reason of the very long journey. And the men took of their victuals and asked not counsel at the mouth of the LORD. And Joshua made peace with them, and made a league with them, to let them live: and the princes of the congregation sware unto them" (**Joshua 9:3-14**) KJV.

The inhabitants of Gibeon were the Hivites who managed to deceive Joshua because of Joshua's failure to inquire from God concerning direction. To avoid being deceived, be sensitive to the Spirit of God, ask for wisdom, and be willing to make tough decisions.

The Jebusites

Associated with self-deception, and overconfidence. The Jebusites believed that Zion was very secured based on their own estimation but did not factor the fact that God was with David nor the supernatural power of God.

"The Jebusites lived in Jerusalem, and David led his army there to attack them. The Jebusites did not think he could get in, so they told him, "You can't get in here! We could run you off, even if we couldn't see or walk!" David told his troops, "You will have to go up through the water tunnel to get those Jebusites. I hate people like them who can't walk or see." That's why there is still a rule that says, "Only people who can walk and see are allowed in the temple." David captured the fortress on Mount Zion, then he moved there and named it David's City. He had the city rebuilt, starting with the landfill to the east. (**Second Samuel 5:6,7**).

The Moabites

Associated with foreign or "strange women", who have been exposed to occult practices and could possibly contaminate Israel with divination, conspiracy, incestuous relationships, fear, and distress.

The Moabites are products of incestuous relationship between father and daughters. They are descendants of the union of Lot and his daughters.

"And they made their father drink wine that night also: and the younger arose and lay with him; and he perceived not when she lay down, nor when she arose. Thus were both the daughters of Lot with child by their father. And the firstborn bare a son, and called his name Moab: the same is the father of the Moabites unto this day. And the younger, she also bare a son, and called his name Benammi: the same is the father of the children of Ammon unto this day" (**Genesis 19:35-37**) KJV.

These "strange women" caused the downfall of Solomon because he chose to ignore God's command regarding marriage with the Canaanites.

"But king Solomon loved many strange women, together with the daughter of Pharaoh, women of the Moabites, Ammonites, Edomites, Zidonians, and Hittites; Of the nations concerning which the LORD said unto the children of Israel, Ye shall not go in to them, neither shall they come in unto you: for surely they will turn away your heart after their gods: Solomon clave unto these in love. And he had seven hundred wives, princesses, and three hundred concubines: and his wives turned away his heart. For it came to pass, when Solomon was old, that his wives turned away his heart after other gods: and his heart was not perfect with the LORD his God, as was the heart of David his father" (**First Kings 11:1-4**) KJV.

The Midianites

The Midianites are descendants of Abraham through one of his wives. Also, Moses married a Midianite for his father-in-law Jethro was a priest of Midian. However, the Midianites became enemies of Israel when they formed alliance with the Moabites against Israel. They did oppress Israel until God delivered Israel through Gideon's leadership.

"The LORD said to Moses, "Treat the Midianites as your enemies, and kill them because they treated you as enemies. They plotted to trick you in the incident that took place at Peor. They used their sister Cozbi, daughter of a Midianite leader, who was killed on the day of the plague caused by the incident at Peor." (**Numbers 25:16-18**) God's Word

The Maonites

The Maonites are also recognized as the inhabitants of Maon and Mount Seir. They have also been identified among others as oppressors of Israel during the time of the Judges.

"The Zidonians also, and the Amalekites, and the Maonites, did oppress you; and ye cried to me, and I delivered you out of their hand" (**Judges 10:12**) KJV.

As a nomadic tribe, they have no fixed location. Figuratively, People with the Maonite spirit usually have no permanent church affiliation. They have no pastoral covering and have the potential for troublemaking before going to the next church.

The Ishmaelites

"And the angel of the LORD said unto her, Behold, thou art with child, and shalt bear a son, and shalt call his name Ishmael, because the LORD hath heard thy affliction. And he will be a wild man; his hand will be against every man, and every man's hand against him; and he shall dwell in the presence of all his brethren" (**Genesis 16:11,12**) KJV.

The patriarch of the Ishmaelites descended from the union of Abraham and an Egyptian maid named Hagar. The union is figurative of the permissive will of God that was initiated by Sarah. Ishmael give birth to twelve sons who fulfilled the prophesy of being a" **wild man; his hand will be against every man."** They are known for slave trades, and some of them wore earrings. The Ishmaelites were half-brother of the Midianites, who are also enemies of Israel.

The Ammonites

"And the younger, she also bare a son, and called his name Benammi: the same is the father of the children of Ammon unto this day." (**Genesis 19:38**) KJV.

Moses in the book of Genesis reveals that the Ammonites are products of incestuous relationship between Lot and his younger daughter who gave birth to Banammi, the progenitor of the Ammonites. They are associated with accusations because the king of the Ammonite accused Israel of trespassing and seizing their land.

"And the king of the children of Ammon answered unto the messengers of Jephthah, Because Israel took away my land, when they came up out of Egypt, from Arnon even unto Jabbok, and unto Jordan: now therefore restore those lands again peaceably" (**Judges 11:13**).

The Amalekites

"Thus, saith the LORD of hosts, I remember that which Amalek did to Israel, how he laid wait for him in the way, when he came up from Egypt. Now go and smite Amalek, and utterly destroy all that they have, and spare them not; but slay both man and woman, infant and suckling, ox and sheep, camel, and ass" (**First Samuel 15:2,3**) KJV.

They were descendants of Amalek who lived in the valley and are known enemies of Israel whom God has used as instrument of divine correction from time to time (**Judges 3:12,13; 6:1-4**). However, King Saul was commanded to destroy the Amalekites and everything associated with them. His partial obedience to God's command became costly.

"And Samuel said unto Saul, I will not return with thee: for thou hast rejected the word of the LORD, and the LORD hath rejected thee from being king over Israel" (**First Samuel 15:26** KJV).

The Hittites

"And Ham, the father of Canaan, saw the nakedness of his father, and told his two brethren without" (**Genesis 9:22** KJV).

The Hittites were descendants of Ham, who exposed Noah's nakedness instead of covering up his father's nakedness which his brothers did. Uriah the Hittite was the first husband of Bathsheba who gave birth to Solomon along with King David as the father.

"And David sent and enquired after the woman. And one said, Is not this Bathsheba, the daughter of Eliam, the wife of Uriah the Hittite?" (**Second Samuel 11:3** KJV).

The Zidonians

"And the children of Israel did evil again in the sight of the LORD, and served Baalim, and Ashtaroth, and the gods of Syria, and the gods of Zidon, and the gods of Moab, and the gods of the children of Ammon, and the gods of the Philistines, and forsook the LORD, and served not him" (**Judges 10:6**).

The Sidonians were the inhabitants of ancient Sidon, that God used as instrument of divine correction (**Judges 10:12**). Solomon's collection of women included at least a Sidonian woman and was negatively influenced by the idol practices of the Zidonians.

"For Solomon went after Ashtoreth the goddess of the Zidonians, and after Milcom the abomination of the Ammonites" (**First Kings 11:5**).

"Because that they have forsaken me, and have worshipped Ashtoreth the goddess of the Zidonians, Chemosh the god of the Moabites, and Milcom the god of the children of Ammon, and have not walked in my ways, to do that which is right in mine eyes, and to keep my statutes and my judgments, as did David his father" (**First Kings 11:33** KJV).

The nation of Sidon however had an important seaport that made it influential in the ancient Phoenician city, now in the modern country of Lebanon.

The Amorites

"And Israel sent messengers unto Sihon king of the Amorites, saying, Let me pass through thy land: we will not turn into the fields, or into the vineyards; we will not drink of the waters of the well: but we will go along by the king's highway, until we be past thy borders. And Sihon would not suffer Israel to pass through his border: but Sihon gathered all his people together and went out against Israel into the wilderness: and he came to Jahaz and fought against Israel. And Israel smote him with the edge of the sword, and possessed his land from Arnon unto Jabbok, even unto the children of Ammon: for the border of the children of Ammon was strong. And Israel took all these cities: and Israel dwelt in all the cities of the Amorites, in Heshbon, and in all the villages thereof. For Heshbon was the city of Sihon the king of the Amorites, who had fought against the former king of Moab, and taken all his land out of his hand, even unto Arnon" (**Numbers 21:21-26**) KJV.

The Amorites were known to be descendants of Canaan and they had an unusually tall people identified as giants (**Amos 2:9**). A famous Amorite King was Sihon refused to give passage to Israel due to suspicion of the Hebrews (**Judges 11:19,20**). The refusal of passage led to war between Israel and the Amorites in which Israel was victorious.

"And Sihon would not suffer Israel to pass through his border: but Sihon gathered all his people together and went out against Israel into the wilderness: and he came to Jahaz, and fought against Israel. And Israel smote him with the edge of the sword, and possessed his land from Arnon unto Jabbok, even unto the children of Ammon: for the border of the children of Ammon was strong. And Israel took all these cities: and Israel dwelt in all the cities of the Amorites, in Heshbon, and in all the villages thereof" (**Numbers 21:23-25** KJV).

The Philistines

The Philistines lived in the area presently known as Gaza strip. They were considered as the enemies of ancient Israel due to the many conflicts between them. The Philistines were credited for the destruction of King Saul and some of his children.

"Now the Philistines fought against Israel; and the men of Israel fled from before the Philistines and fell down slain in mount Gilboa. And the Philistines followed hard after Saul, and after his sons; and the Philistines slew Jonathan, and Abinadab, and Malchishua, the sons of Saul. And the battle went sore against Saul, and the archers hit him, and he was wounded of the archers. Then said Saul to his armourbearer, Draw thy sword, and thrust me through therewith; lest these uncircumcised come and abuse me. But his armourbearer would not; for he was sore afraid. So, Saul took a sword, and fell upon it" (**First Chronicles 10:1-4**) KJV.

However, David brought victory to Israel in an earlier conflict with the killing of Philistine military commander named Goliath.

"And it came to pass, when the Philistine arose, and came and drew nigh to meet David, that David hasted, and ran toward the army to meet the Philistine. And David put his hand in his bag, and took thence a stone, and slang it, and smote the Philistine in his forehead, that the stone sunk into his forehead; and he fell upon his face to the earth. So, David prevailed over the Philistine with a sling and with a stone, and smote the Philistine, and slew him; but there was no sword in the hand of David. Therefore, David ran, and stood upon the Philistine, and took his sword, and drew it out of the sheath thereof, and slew him, and cut off his head therewith. And when the Philistines saw their champion was dead, they fled" (**First Samuel 17:48-51** KJV).

About The Author
Bishop George O. Adebanjo

Bishop George O. Adebanjo, Th.D. is the Pastor and Founder of The Living Word International Church of God in Christ located in Nashville, TN. He is a native of Lagos, Nigeria where he received his primary and secondary education. He received both the Master's and Doctorate degrees in theology (M.Th. and Th.D.) from Andersonville Theological Seminary in Camilla, Georgia, a Bachelor of Science (BS) in Mechanical Engineering from Tennessee State University in Nashville, TN and a Stationary Engineer's license from George Brown College of Applied Arts & Technology in Toronto Canada.

His license and degree in Engineering opened many doors of opportunity for professional advancement. He has worked professionally at some of Nashville's most distinguished universities, inclusive of Meharry Medical College and Fisk University. In his professional role, he established his own engineering company, ADE Engineering and Management Services, Inc (AEMS). He likewise founded the Nashville Chapter of the Association of Energy Engineers, whose membership comprised some of Tennessee's most prominent firms, companies, and institutions.

In 1994, Bishop Adebanjo took a giant step of faith and walked away from a professional career in engineering to passionately pursue the call of God into a life of full-time ministry. He has literally traveled extensively to many parts of the world sharing the Word of God, maintaining a community and global vision to advance the gospel to the ends of the earth.

In 2005, because of Pastor Adebanjo's diligence and undeniable effectiveness in ministry worldwide, he was consecrated as Bishop of Pakistan by the presidium of The Church of God In Christ Inc., under the leadership of the late Bishop Gilbert Earl Patterson.

Bishop Adebanjo is not only known to be an anointed and dynamic pastor, teacher, and evangelist but also a visionary. As such, he has established several outreach organizations and has taken ministry beyond the walls of the church and into the local and global communities. Through International Outreach Ministries Inc., Bishop

Adebanjo has provided assistance and services both locally and internationally through such programs as the neighborhood witnessing program, a church-based food bank and feeding program, an emergency shelter for the homeless, job training programs, a grade school tutorial program, summer enrichment programs, prison outreach and education, HIV outreach and education, and the support of orphanages in Africa.

Being a firm believer in community involvement, Bishop Adebanjo is affiliated with several board memberships and non-profit organizations. He is a song writer and author of several books, inclusive of: Thank God for Deliverance; No Weapon Formed Shall Prevail; The Cost of Worship; Fasting with a Purpose; and Discerning Spiritual Attacks. He is also known locally as a television and radio personality having hosted and produced several radio and television programs as well as having made several guest appearances on the Trinity Broadcast Network (TBN) and Christian Broadcast Network CBN).

Bishop Adebanjo's heartbeat for the nations has been the impetus behind his global travels spreading the gospel of Jesus Christ, planting churches and providing apostolic covering for many churches and pastors, particularly in Asia and Africa. Thousands have been saved, healed and delivered as a result.

He is married to Dr. Jennifer W. Adebanjo, Associate Professor of Political Science and Chair of the History and Political Science Department at the prestigious Fisk University in Nashville. He has one daughter and one grandson.

Bibliography

Demonology (Past And Present) Kurt Koch

Google Search

Annihilating The Hosts Of Hell! Win Worley

Christianity In Crisis: Sun Myung Moon

Dake's Annotated Reference; Finis Hennings Dake

Drought In Africa: Michael H. Glantz,

Scientific American, June 1987, Vol. 1256 No. 6

Earth; Presider

Ebony, Death Stalks West Africa. Carl T. Rowan

He Came To Set The Captives Free; Rebecca Brown, M.D.

Heroines Of Service Mary Rosetta Parkman

Joshua And Judges; J. Vernon Mcgee

Jerusalem-The Tragedy And The Triump;P Charles Gulston

Miracle Seed Of Faith; Oral Roberts

Neewswatch; Death Fiesta, March 27, 1989 Abdulrazaq Magaji

Newsweek; The Search For Adam And Eve, Jan. 11,1988 John
Tierney, Lynda Wright, Karen Springen

Power And Influence; An Introduction To International Relations;
D.G. Kousolas

Racism And The Church: A Report-Lutheran Church, Missouri Synod

Scofield Reference Bible

Smith's Bible Dictionary; Dr. William Smith

Strong's Concordance: Hebrew/Greek/English

The Amplified Bible

The Breast To The Earth: Kofi Awooner

The Edge Of Evil: Jerry Johnson

The First Book Of Africa: Langston Hughes

The Interpreter's Bible Vol. 11 Abingdon

The New Lexicon Webster's Dictionary: Deluxe Encyclopedic Edition

The New Manners An Dcustoms Of The Bible Times: Ralph Gower

The Revelation Of John: Exposition By Charles R. Erdran
The Rsv Interlinear Greek-English New Testament: Alfred Marshall
The Three Battlegrounds- Francis Frangipane

Made in the USA
Columbia, SC
09 September 2024

41340161R00076